Heptameron
Circles of Presence

Luan Ferr

*A Complete Guide to the Conjuration of Angels
According to the Ceremonial Magic of Solomon*

Original Title: *Heptameron – Círculos da Presença*

Copyright © 2025, published by Luiz Antonio dos Santos ME. This book is a work of non-fiction that explores practices and concepts in the field of Christian ceremonial magic. Through a progressive and profound approach, the author offers detailed ritual instructions for the conjuration of angels according to the Solomonic tradition, contextualizing its use for the modern operator based on the grimoire *Heptameron* attributed to Pietro d'Abano.

1st Edition**Production Team**
Author: Luan Ferr
Translation: Edivaldo Ferreira
Editor: Luiz Santos
Cover: Studios Booklas / Elian Marquet
Consultant: Alverin Dosk
Researchers: Ralen Mirko / Tessa Vonel / Merid Arkon
Layout: Jalif Tenari
Publication and Identification
Heptameron – Circles of Presence Booklas, 2025
Categories: Ceremonial Magic / Esoteric Spirituality
DDC: 133.43 – **UDC:** 133.5
All rights reserved to:
Luiz Antonio dos Santos ME / Booklas No part of this book may be reproduced, stored in a retrieval system, or transmitted in any form or by any means—electronic, mechanical, photocopying, recording, or otherwise—without the prior express written permission of the copyright holder.

Editorial Presentation

It is with great respect for tradition and a profound sense of spiritual responsibility that we deliver this carefully crafted work to the reader: a complete and progressive guide to the ritualistic practice described in the *Heptameron*, attributed to Pietro d'Abano. Throughout the centuries, this singular grimoire has evoked fascination, awe, and veneration for containing detailed instructions for the conjuration of celestial intelligences and ceremonial magic operations under a deeply symbolic and Christian framework.

Unlike mere translations or transcriptions of ancient manuscripts, this book aims to be a living bridge between the classic text and the modern practitioner. To this end, we have organized the content into sixteen didactic and progressive chapters that guide the reader from a theoretical introduction to the practical execution of the rites, including instructions on preparation, astrological calculations, operative ethics, and models for ritual recording.

The approach adopted seeks to balance textual fidelity, pedagogical clarity, and spiritual depth. Each chapter was written with the intent of preserving the spirit of the Solomonic tradition, but without losing sight of the needs of the contemporary operator—who often lacks not only precise instructions but also a moral and psychic context to sustain the potency of the rite.

We have included, at the end, a visual and practical appendix with tables, Latin translations, seals, and complementary instructions. This material aims to facilitate the concrete application of the described operations, allowing the book to function not only as an object of study but as a complete and functional ritualistic instrument.

This volume is not intended for superficial curiosity, nor for frivolous experimentation. It speaks to the sincere heart of those who seek knowledge, transformation, and communion with the sacred through the ceremonial path. The *Heptameron*, though small in length, demands maturity, humility, and reverence. Its power lies not only in the names it invokes but in the internal vibration with which they are pronounced.

For this reason, we reiterate: magical practice is inseparable from ethics and consciousness. Every ritual is also a mirror. Every evocation is a call to one's own soul. May this book, then, serve as a map and a mirror; as a key and a reminder; as an invitation and a consecration.

With wishes of light, balance, and discernment along the journey,

Luiz Santos, Editor

Table of Content

Editorial Presentation 3
Chapter 1 The Grimoire Heptameron 6
Chapter 2 Preparation of the Initiate 17
Chapter 3 The Three Magic Circles 35
Chapter 4 The Operator's Tools 53
Chapter 5 Blessing of the Circle 75
Chapter 6 Blessing of the Perfumes 92
Chapter 7 Exorcism of the Fire 113
Chapter 8 The Seven Days and Their Angels 130
Chapter 9 Magical Hours and Seasons 154
Chapter 10 Preparing the Conjuration Ritual 173
Chapter 11 The Invocation of the Angels 192
Chapter 12 Communication and Petition 210
Chapter 13 The Ritual Farewell 229
Chapter 14 Records and Post-Ritual Care 246
Chapter 15 Ethics and Dangers of the Art 260
Chapter 16 Visual Appendix and Tables 275
Afterword 280

Chapter 1
The Grimoire Heptameron

When we delve into the ancient grimoires of the Western tradition, we discover that they were not conceived as mere repositories of enchantments, but as ritual maps for the soul. The *Heptameron*, in this sense, is no exception: it is a spiritual artifact whose liturgical and symbolic sophistication reveals a profound search for meaning, for communion with celestial forces, and for inner transformation. Attributed to Pietro d'Abano, a multifaceted figure who moved between medicine, philosophy, and astrology, this grimoire organizes the liturgical time of magic with precision and reverence. The cycle of the seven days—each ruled by a planetary archangel—is not an arbitrary convention but a reflection of the cosmic order inscribed in the very fabric of the world.

Each day of the week is, therefore, a window to a distinct spiritual quality, mediated by entities representing the planetary spheres. The practices of the *Heptameron* were designed not only to summon these presences but to attune the operator to the invisible rhythm of the cosmos, realigning their body, mind, and spirit with a higher hierarchy. This requires more than technical knowledge: it demands a state of inner purity and a sincere engagement with the mysteries. Evocation, in this system, is not a tool for domination, but a gesture of humility before the sacred, an attempt to listen and collaborate with intelligences that transcend common experience.

The weekly structure of the *Heptameron*—seven days, seven archangels, seven rituals—echoes a worldview in which time is not linear, but cyclical and consecrated. Monday is dedicated to the Moon and the archangel Gabriel, whose attributes involve dreams, revelations, and the world of emotions. Tuesday belongs to Mars and Samael, with an emphasis on courage and just action. And so on, until the solar Sunday, ruled by Michael, the warrior archangel of light and truth. Each day, the magician approaches a facet of the divine, gradually integrating these aspects into their own being.

In addition to astrological correspondences, the *Heptameron* offers detailed instructions on vestments, canonical hours, appropriate incenses, the directions to be faced, and the names to be pronounced. It is a system that seeks fidelity to tradition and, at the same time, spiritual efficacy. The use of sacred names, for example, is not intended to manipulate the divine but to invoke its presence with reverence. Each name carries within it a specific vibration, a spiritual signature that resonates with the higher spheres. To utter them correctly is a form of attunement, as if each word opened a door between worlds.

The weekly practice proposed by the *Heptameron* can be seen as a cosmic rosary: each day is a bead on the thread of eternity, and the operator, by traversing them with intention, transforms the ordinary into a sacrament. It is a magical liturgy that does not oppose religion but proposes an inner priesthood, where the temple is the purified body itself, the altar is the magic circle, and the prayer is the call to the divine presence. In this process, everyday time is transfigured—it becomes *kairos*, sacred time, a time for listening.

In a world that often dissociates spirituality from concrete practice, the *Heptameron* stands as a bridge between theory and experience. It does not promise immediate results, nor does it offer shortcuts to power. On the contrary, it demands constancy, patience, and an ethic of intention. Its value lies precisely in restoring to magic its sacred character, re-establishing a path of access to the invisible dimension that sustains and permeates reality. And that is why, centuries after its creation, it continues to inspire serious seekers—not as a relic of the past, but as a living school of the spirit.

The text instructs the operator to draw magic circles, prepare specific clothes and instruments, perform consecrations, bless perfumes and fire, and finally invoke the angels with solemn prayers and formulas. All of this must be done with ritualistic precision, reverent faith, and a clear spiritual intention. The literal and symbolic execution of these steps is a fundamental part of success in spiritual manifestation, since the ritual not only invites celestial beings but also transforms the operator internally.

The *Heptameron* stands out for presenting a self-contained and practical system of Christian ceremonial magic. Unlike grimoires dedicated exclusively to the invocation of spirits or demons, this work is focused on the evocation of celestial entities. Its prayers are addressed to God, its seals are associated with divine names, and its ultimate purpose is to elevate the human spirit through ritual experience and communion with angels. It is a practice that demands reverence and cannot be conducted lightly or motivated by vanity.

At the core of the *Heptameron* lies an implicit theology that rejects the separation between magic and sanctity. It is a work that inscribes magical practice within a Christ-centered horizon, where the operator, far from acting as a usurper of forces, positions themselves as a liturgical officiant in a spiritual drama that repeats, in miniature, the architecture of the cosmos. The evocation of angels, in this context, is not a form of control, but of listening and receptivity. It is as if the operator were setting a symbolic table and calling the celestial guests, not to dominate them, but to commune with their presence and learn from their wisdom.

This profoundly devotional character distinguishes the *Heptameron* from other magical traditions of the same era. Instead of formulas that promise immediate power or pragmatic results, it offers a spiritual itinerary. The operator seeks not only to transform external reality, but rather to undergo an internal refinement that makes them worthy of receiving angelic influxes. Thus, the true result of the practice is not a visible prodigy, but a silent transfiguration, often imperceptible to the eyes of the world, but radical within.

This approach also imposes a rigorous ethos on the practitioner. The preparation is not only ritualistic but moral: it requires humility, restraint of desires, and a sincere abandonment of vanities. The magician must cultivate patience and purity, for the angelic presence, according to the *Heptameron*, does not manifest in the face of irreverence or superficiality. It demands a heart prepared like fertile ground—free from arrogance, clean of dubious intentions.

The liturgy of the grimoire is, in this sense, a pedagogy of the spirit. Each seal, each name, each ritualized gesture has the function of attuning the operator's body and soul to the hidden music of the spheres. The symbolic ensemble acts as a mirror: it reveals to the practitioner that which in them resists the light, that which cannot yet be touched without harm. And for this very reason, the *Heptameron* is not a manual of mechanical practices, but a living book that responds to the maturity of the one who consults it.

There is also an austere beauty in its conception: everything is codified, measured, sacred. Nothing is improvised, for everything echoes a higher order. The practice becomes an offering—not only of words but of full attention. In a time when haste governs even the sacred, the *Heptameron* insists on another rhythm: that of contemplation, of fidelity, of the silence that precedes listening.

Therefore, to evoke the angels according to this grimoire is not to seek a spectacle of lights, but to align oneself with a tradition that understands the invisible as a living reality, sensitive to the ethics and intention of the operator. And it is this fidelity to the invisible—more than any immediate result—that transforms the practice into a path of ascesis. The *Heptameron* is not a door to power, but a threshold to the sacred. Whoever crosses it, with reverence and truth, discovers that to conjure is, above all, to become worthy of being heard.

The work can be divided into several fundamental sections:

- Preparation of the operator: requires physical purification, fasting, prayer, and specific vestments. The magician must also observe moral precepts, keep their mind free from impure thoughts, and establish a sincere commitment to truth.
- Construction of the magic circles: three concentric circles with divine names, angels, and symbols corresponding to the time of the ritual. These circles are drawn with chalk, charcoal, or a ritual wand, always in an isolated, clean, and consecrated place.
- Consecrations and blessings: lustral water, perfumes, incenses, and sacred fire are blessed for ritual use. Nothing enters the magical space without being purified and dedicated to divine service.
- Evocation by day of the week: each day brings a specific set of entities, prayers, and seals. The magician needs to know the planetary rulership and the intelligences of the air associated with each day.

- Instructions for closing: dismissal of the entities, purification of the space, and post-ritual recommendations. This final phase is as important as the beginning, as it seals the integrity of the work.

This structure aims to create a ritually pure and spiritually protected environment so that the celestial intelligences can manifest visibly within the magic circle. It is not theater, but an operative reality based on the harmony between intention, rite, and sacred symbology.

It is important to understand that the *Heptameron* is not a grimoire of black magic or deviant occultism. On the contrary: it invokes the authority of God, Christ, and the holy angels, using prayers based on excerpts from the Bible and Catholic liturgy. The practices demand reverence, faith, and spiritual commitment. It is a priestly art, where the operator assumes a role analogous to that of a liturgical officiant, often reciting psalms, chanting hymns, and handling consecrated instruments with specific ritual gestures.

The objective of the practices may be to obtain wisdom, healing, spiritual protection, revelations, or help for other people. It is not about imposing personal wills on the spiritual world, but about attuning with higher intelligences to collaborate with the designs of good. The magician becomes, in this context, a servant of the divine, not a master of the invisible.

Furthermore, the *Heptameron* promotes the development of essential spiritual virtues: patience, humility, discipline, discernment, and devotion. Each ritual is a lesson in listening, concentration, and presence. The visible manifestation of a spirit is only one of the fruits; the most important is the inner transformation of the practitioner themself.

The visible manifestation of angels and spirits requires the operator to prepare a consecrated space, symbolically ordered and energetically clean. The magic circle, in this context, is not just a protective barrier—it is a living altar, a terrestrial mandala that reflects the celestial order. It serves as a landing point for the spiritual presences that respond to the operator's call.

The drawing of the circle should be done on clean ground, preferably on a white cloth, in a silent place. The interior of the circle is adorned with the sacred names of God—for example, Adonai, Tetragrammaton, El, Elohim—interspersed with crosses. In its center, Alpha and Omega are written, and four divine names are placed in the cardinal quadrants.

Every element that constitutes the ritual has a purpose: the perfumes elevate the vibration of the environment; the sacred fire purifies; the holy water exorcises unwanted forces; the divine names establish authority and connection with the angelic hierarchies. The conjuration, then, is not a supernatural spectacle, but a symbolic language of communion. The practice of the circle teaches the operator that the invisible is not accessed by brute force, but by order, harmony, and reverence.

In a time when many turn away from profound spiritual practices due to ignorance or disbelief, the *Heptameron* presents itself as a bridge between tradition and modernity. It offers a structured, devotional, and effective path for reconnection with the sacred. It does not demand submission to an institutional religion but proposes discipline, clear intention, and respect for higher forces. In a noisy world, it offers ritual silence. Amidst modern dispersion, it proposes sacred focus.

The modern practitioner can use the *Heptameron* as an instrument of inner transformation, as a method of spiritual assistance to others, or as a contemplative path of contact with the invisible worlds. Its language is symbolic, but its effects are concrete for those who practice it with seriousness and humility. The rituals of the *Heptameron* function as windows that open between the planes—and the operator, provided they are prepared, becomes a conscious mediator between the worlds.

This first movement aims not only to inform but to prepare the spirit for a type of reading that is also a practice of attention. What is presented here is not a succession of historical data or technical instructions, but an introduction to a field where symbols, gestures, and words form a sacred language. To approach the *Heptameron* with this awareness means recognizing that every element contained in its pages is a key—and that these keys only perform their function before a willing heart, a concentrated mind, and a purified body.

There is, in the composition of the grimoire, an architecture that demands more than intellectual understanding: it requires experiential assimilation. What has been outlined so far is a cartography of the sacred, a sketch of the inner temple that the operator must build with their own acts, thoughts, and intentions. Nothing described is fortuitous: the days, the angels, the names, the rites, all point to a higher order that wishes to be re-actualized through practice. Magic, in this context, is not an end, but a means—a way by which the human being remembers their celestial origin and, at the same time, purifies themself to rediscover it.

The path suggested here is neither one of vague mysticism nor of superficial religiosity. It is, rather, that of an intimate, silent priesthood, in which every detail is an expression of surrender. The sacred names should not just be pronounced: they need to be heard from within, as if the soul itself were speaking them. The circle drawn on the ground is not just a boundary: it is the mirror of an order that the world has forgotten. And the evoked archangels are not characters: they are real presences that allow themselves to be perceived only when there is truth in the call.

Thus, this beginning already carries within it the spirit of what is to come: it is not about acquiring formulas or collecting seals, but about entering a process of inner refinement. The path is demanding, but generous. Each step, when taken with sincere intention, reveals more than was promised. And if there is something to be gained, it is not dominion over external forces, but the capacity to become a worthy vessel for the light that permeates all things. What opens here is not a path of dominion, but a road of listening. And to listen, in this universe, is to allow the sacred to speak—not only through the angels, but through every gesture, every word, and every silence that the operator consecrates on their journey.

Chapter 2
Preparation of the Initiate

The ladder of conjuration, like any authentic spiritual path, does not begin with an external gesture, but in inner silence. Before the operator draws any circle on the ground, a circle of intention and purity must first be drawn within. The *Heptameron* is not a book for the curious or the skeptical—it is a sacred tool intended for those who sincerely wish to move between worlds. This chapter is, therefore, a summons. A summons to presence, reverence, and preparation. Without this foundation, no ritual will have true power.

This summons does not demand perfection, but wholeness. It requires the initiate to be willing to suspend, even for a brief time, the voices of the world and the masks of daily life to immerse themselves in deep listening. It is a call that resonates not in the ears, but in the center of being, where the desire for truth still pulses amidst the ashes of modern distraction. The first step on the ladder is the sincere willingness to be silent in order to listen, to empty oneself in order to receive. This is not about dogma or imposition, but about inner posture: those who approach the sacred with arrogance or levity will find nothing but the echo of their own confusion.

In the silence before the rite, resistance often arises—restless thoughts, unresolved memories, dormant anxieties. This discomfort is not a sign of failure, but of purification. Preparation requires the courage to cross the shadow that separates the mundane from the luminous. Just as gold must pass through fire to reveal its purity, the operator's spirit must pass through the crucible of silence and vigilance.

This inner process can manifest in various ways: a subtle restlessness upon engaging with the text of the *Heptameron*, an inexplicable need for retreat, or even symbolic dreams that seem to reorganize the unconscious. These are all signs that the summons has been heard, even if partially. What is asked for, from then on, is continuity. True spirituality does not flourish in sporadic acts, but in consistent, albeit simple, gestures.

In preparing for the rite, the initiate seeks not only spiritual power, but purification. The act of conjuring, in the profound sense of the term, is a mutual call: by evoking a higher intelligence, the operator also allows themselves to be evoked by it, becoming both receptacle and offering. The circle drawn on the ground should not be merely a protective barrier; it is a mirror of the invisible circle that must be established in the heart—one where doubt, pride, or the desire for control cannot enter.

This preparation, therefore, is a process of attunement. Like an instrument that must be finely tuned for sacred music to manifest, the initiate needs to harmonize their various aspects so that the spiritual presence, when it comes, finds a dwelling place and not resistance. Many wonder why their rites fail or seem empty—and, most of the time, it is because the inner altar is in ruins, even if the physical altar is impeccable.

To be prepared is more than knowing what to do. It is to be present in what one does, with reverence and listening. It is to renounce haste and the desire for immediate results to enter a sacred time, where every gesture has weight and every word, density. It is knowing that the true magical work does not begin with the invocation, but long before it—at the moment the operator decides, with humility, to become a living channel between the worlds.

Thus, the ladder of conjuration is built not just with formulas or seals, but with continuous presence. And presence is born from preparation. Therefore, before seeking the names of angels, it is necessary to invoke one's own wholeness. Before lighting the candle, one must ignite the spirit. Before any rite, there must be the profound "yes" of one who wishes not only to see miracles, but to become worthy of them.

To prepare, in the context of the *Heptameron*, is to align the three levels of being—body, mind, and spirit—so that they become a cohesive channel through which the evoked spiritual intelligence can manifest. The operator is the link between Earth and Heaven. Their preparation is not merely symbolic: it is functional. An impure body, a scattered mind, or a disharmonious soul become direct obstacles to angelic manifestation. Therefore, each step must be followed with attention, dedication, and purpose.

1. Physical Preparation

The body is the temple of action. It must be clean, rested, lightly nourished, and free of toxins. It is recommended:

2. Light fasting for the 12 hours preceding the ritual. Water and herbal infusions are permitted, while avoiding meat, alcohol, and heavy or processed foods. This fast is not merely physical: by reducing digestive activity, the body redirects its energy to the subtler senses, sharpening perception and facilitating expanded states of consciousness. The fast, therefore, is a silent pedagogy of opening. It is not about deprivation, but about space: inner space for the sacred to enter.

3. A purification bath, with coarse salt and herbs such as rosemary, rue, or lavender. During the bath, the operator can recite Psalm 51 (*Miserere mei, Deus*) as a prayer for inner cleansing. This ritual bath is not an empty symbolic gesture. It acts on the energetic body, dissolving accumulated densities and restoring the harmonious flow between the subtle centers. The coarse salt has the role of absorbing miasmas and psychic residues, while the herbs elevate the field's vibration. Reciting a psalm at this moment is to imprint direction and intention upon the water, transforming it into a vehicle of grace.

4. Ritual attire: a simple white tunic of cotton or linen, without symbols or adornments. This garment represents neutrality and consecration. It should be used only for rituals and kept with respect. By dressing in it, the operator silently declares that they are no longer in ordinary time, but in the time of the rite. The tunic

becomes a mantle of transition, an intermediate skin between the profane world and the sacred space. Keeping it apart, in a reserved place, is to acknowledge its role as a garment of passage.

5. A quiet bodily environment: avoid sexuality, intense noise, and mundane conversations for at least 24 hours before the rite. The body needs to "slow down" to become receptive. This includes avoiding agitated music, arguments, excessive use of electronics, and other stimuli that disturb the inner frequency. Silence is not the absence of sound, but the presence of listening. By abstaining from stimuli, the body begins to vibrate at another rhythm, one closer to the spiritual. Every movement becomes more conscious, every breath, deeper.

This purification of the body is not empty asceticism. It is preparation to become a receptacle for a high presence. The body is the first dwelling to be put in order. And this ordering is not done with rigidity or denial, but with respect. By caring for the body with this intention, the initiate learns that matter is not an obstacle to the spirit, but its ally. The body, when well-prepared, becomes as sensitive as a tuned instrument, capable of perceiving invisible nuances, sustaining elevated energies, and translating into gestures what the spirit intuits. It is in this body, now a temple, that the sacred can manifest with truth.

6. Psychological Preparation

The mind is the mirror of the ritual practice. No angel will manifest to a spirit immersed in distractions. Therefore, it is necessary to cultivate:

- Inner silence: avoid television, social media, news, or excessive external stimuli on the day of the ritual. The mind should be collected, not scattered. This withdrawal is not isolation, but recalibration. By silencing the informational noise that floods daily life, the operator allows their thoughts to slow down and their perception to become more transparent. It is about preparing a field of deep listening, where intuition can emerge without being stifled by mental chatter. Inner silence is like a lake that, when peaceful, clearly reflects the light of the sky.
- Prior study: know the names, psalms, and seals that will be used, so that nothing is read with hesitation or unfamiliarity during the rite. Familiarity with the ritual elements is not for the sake of erudition, but for fluidity. When the operator knows what they will utter, their word acquires power and their gesture becomes complete. The mind, then, does not stumble on doubt or forgetfulness—it firmly holds the guiding thread of the operation. Prior study is an act of reverence for that which one wishes to invoke: no one enters a sacred temple with ignorance or haste.
- Daily meditation, for at least 10 to 15 minutes, in the week prior. One can meditate by visualizing a white light descending from the top of the head to the heart, harmonizing thoughts. This simple practice creates a bridge between the conscious and the subtle, weans the mind from distraction,

and introduces it to the space of attention. The image of the descending white light is not merely symbolic: it activates internal circuits of pacification and grounding. The heart, the center of spiritual consciousness, becomes the throne of attention—and the mind, instead of being dominant, learns to serve the spirit.

- Review of intentions: write down clearly and sincerely why one wishes to perform that ritual. Intention is the spiritual seed of the outcome. By writing down their motivations, the operator purifies their desires, identifies contaminations of the ego, and confronts their true needs. This review is often the most revealing moment of the entire preparation. Vague intentions generate confused results; clear intentions, even if humble, attract precise answers. Therefore, it is recommended that the initiate write their intentions by hand, in a ritual notebook, as one who sows a field with attention and faith.

The mind, when trained, becomes a clear mirror where the invisible can be reflected. Without this clarity, the rite becomes a mechanical repetition, and the spiritual presence finds resistance instead of welcome. Psychological preparation does not require genius, but discipline. It requires the daily choice not to be distracted, not to become dull, not to surrender the space of the mind to daily chaos. Over time, this discipline becomes natural. And the naturalness of a serene mind is one of the safest doors to the sacred.

7. Spiritual Preparation

The deepest part of the preparation is the spiritual one. The *Heptameron* works with elevated entities that respond to the call of the spirit, not the ego. For this:

- Daily prayer: prayers such as the Lord's Prayer, the Invocation of the Holy Spirit, or specific psalms for purification (Psalm 23, 51, or 91) are suggested. These prayers should not be recited mechanically, but with attention and reverence, as if they were letters addressed to the invisible world. Each well-pronounced word acts as a seal of light that seals the heart against distraction. Daily prayer prepares the operator's vibrational field, making them gradually more attuned to the higher planes. It trains presence, purifies intention, and anchors humility.
- Inner confession: if there are grievances, guilt, or unresolved attitudes, one must acknowledge them and ask for forgiveness—from oneself, from God, and from those involved. The magician must be at peace with their heart. This is not a religious ritual, but a matter of inner integrity. Any emotional residue carried into the rite distorts the purity of the call. Therefore, the sincere recognition of faults, true repentance, and an honest desire for amends form a magnetic field conducive to spiritual manifestation. It is in this emptying of guilt and bitterness that the spirit can rise lightly.
- Spiritual fasting: abstain from vain words, judgment of others, criticism, and

discouragement. Feed the spirit with beauty, truth, and charity. This type of fasting is often more demanding than the physical one, as it implies continuous vigilance over the ego's impulses. It consists of not responding to the world with reactivity, but with presence; of not reproducing patterns of negativity, but cultivating discreet virtues. A calm, generous heart, clean of vanities, becomes fertile ground where the angel can tread.

- Symbolic offering: light a white candle for seven days before the first operation, asking for light and discernment from your guardian angel. This simple gesture is a way of anticipating the rite, like sending an invitation to the celestial world. The flame of the candle, renewed each day, represents the initiate's commitment to their own purification and to the truth of what they will ask. During these seven days, it is recommended that the operator maintain an attitude of recollection, meditating briefly before the candle and renewing their request in silence.

This spiritual preparation transforms the ritual into a living and authentic offering. It ensures that the external gesture—no matter how precise and well-executed—is not empty. When the spirit is aligned with the intention, when there is truth in the quest and humility in the gesture, the invisible responds with clarity. It is this spiritual purity that separates the true operator from the mere executor of formulas. It is what confers density, presence, and power to the rite, making it not a spectacle, but an encounter.

8. The Practice Space

Before any circle is drawn, the space must be chosen and prepared:
- A quiet and private environment, where there will be no interruptions or the presence of animals during the ritual. This withdrawal of the external space reflects the need for a symbolic separation between the ordinary and the sacred world. The place of practice should be a threshold—an in-between place where the energies from above can descend without interference. Silence, here, means more than the absence of noise: it is the creation of an atmosphere of respect, where every element present participates in the rite with discretion and harmony.
- A clean floor, preferably of stone, wood, or on a consecrated white cloth. The floor is the base upon which the magic circle will be raised, and its cleanliness should be not only physical but also vibrational. Some operators sprinkle lustral water or use light smudging to purify the surface. The white cloth functions as a veil that separates the ritual space from the profane world, a kind of horizontal altar upon which the sacred can rest.
- Soft light: the environment should be illuminated with candles, avoiding direct artificial light. The light of fire connects the rite to the ancestral tradition of living altars. Its natural flicker and subtle warmth invite the spirit to presence and help the operator enter a state of expanded attention. Artificial light is avoided as it interferes

with energetic sensitivity and the creation of a conducive ambiance. Each lit candle is a silent call to the invisible presence.
- Purifying aromas, such as frankincense or sandalwood incense, burned before the practice to prepare the atmosphere. The sense of smell is one of the most direct pathways to the nervous system and symbolic memory. Burning appropriate incenses elevates the vibration of the space and acts as an olfactory invitation to the spiritual presence. It is recommended that the incense be natural, of good quality, and that its smoke travel through the environment in slow circles, almost as if dancing with the space. The operator can accompany the smudging with prayers, chants, or attentive silence.

If possible, the space should be used only for spiritual practices. If this is not feasible, a white curtain or a circle symbolically demarcated with crystals can isolate the place from profane daily life. This symbolic separation is fundamental: it teaches the body and mind that this place, however modest, is now sacred territory. The simple act of demarcating the space already constitutes a first magical gesture. Each time the operator enters this environment, their body will recognize the vibration, their breathing will adjust, and their mind will be naturally led to the state of ritual attention.

9. The Inner Altar

There is no effective *Heptameron* without an inner altar. The physical altar may contain:

- A central white candle
- A crucifix or divine symbol
- A chalice with lustral water
- An incense burner
- The grimoire or text with the seals and prayers

These elements are not decorative, but living instruments that condense, evoke, and sustain the spiritual presence. Each has a precise function: the candle, as the spark of the soul; the divine symbol, as an anchor of intention; the water, as a channel of purification; the incense, as a subtle offering; the grimoire, as a map of access to the invisible. Their arrangement should follow an intuitive, harmonious, and always respectful order.

But the true altar is the inner disposition of the operator. To sit before a clean altar, if the heart is impure, is like dressing in light while carrying darkness within. The magician must approach the work with reverent awe, as one who treads on sacred ground. This awe is not fear, but a recognition of the greatness with which one is coming into contact. Each time the operator lights the candle, raises the chalice, or opens the grimoire, they are saying: "I am here. Here I am." And this disposition, when genuine, is what transforms a simple space into an altar and a simple gesture into a sacrament.

10. Time, Seasons, and Rhythm

The *Heptameron* is a grimoire deeply connected to the cycles of nature, planetary hours, and the seasons of the year. Therefore, the operator must learn to:

- Observe the right day: each rite is associated with a day of the week and a celestial ruler. This correspondence is not arbitrary: it reflects a profound harmony between astral movements and the spiritual qualities evoked in each operation. For example, Monday's rites, under the regency of the Moon, favor work with intuition, memories, and hidden revelations. Thursday's rites, under Jupiter, are ideal for invoking wisdom, expansion, and justice. Choosing the correct day is to align with the cosmic flow and allow it to work in favor of the rite, not against it.
- Choose the correct magical hour: using astrological tables, planetary hour apps, or manual calculations. Each day contains seven planetary cycles that follow a fixed order, and each hour carries the vibrational signature of the planet that rules it. Starting a ritual in the hour of Mars, for example, imparts vigor and intensity to the operation, while the hour of Venus favors harmony and conciliation. By precisely identifying the appropriate hour, the operator creates a cohesive temporal field, where the evoked spiritual presence finds resonance and welcome.
- Pay attention to the season of the year, as the grimoire mentions that some names and sigils vary with the seasons. Celestial forces do not manifest in the same way at all times of the year. Summer carries an expansive and solar energy; winter, a withdrawal conducive to introspection

and purification. Spring renews, autumn unveils what needs to die. Each season shapes the invisible backdrop upon which the rite will be inscribed. An attentive operator will be able to observe how certain symbols reveal themselves more clearly in certain months, how dreams and signs intensify according to the Earth's cycle. This cyclical listening transforms the operator into a reader of time, and not just of words.

- Synchronize with the Moon: lunar phases influence the energy of the rite (the waxing moon favors expansion; the waning, cleansing). The Moon acts as a bridge between the visible and the invisible, between the physical world and the animic world. Its presence, though silent, directly affects the efficacy of the operations. The new moon is ideal for planting new intentions; the full moon, for consecrations and revelations. During the waning moon, practices of banishment, release, and purification gain potency. The initiate who regularly observes the Moon becomes, little by little, intimate with the rhythm of the soul— and the rite becomes more than an isolated event: it becomes part of a dance between heaven, earth, and spirit.

The operator becomes a "priest of time," not someone who fights against it. This priesthood of time does not require advanced astrological knowledge, but attention and respect. Each temporal choice is a gesture of alignment with something greater, a way of saying: "I do not command, I cooperate." And it is in this gesture that true magic flourishes—not as an imposition of will, but as co-creation with the eternal rhythms.

11. Dialogue with the Invisible

By preparing with seriousness, the reader begins to perceive that the rite is not just about seeing or hearing angels—but about learning to listen to them with the heart. The invisible speaks in subtleties: a dream, an intuition, an internal change after the rite.

This listening is not achieved through curiosity, but through presence. The true dialogue with the invisible is built in silence, humility, and persistence. It is neither immediate nor spectacular. On the contrary, it manifests gradually, like a subtle perfume that is only noticed when the body becomes still. The attentive initiate will notice that certain thoughts become clearer after an invocation, that previously confusing decisions become illuminated with spontaneous discernment. It is these small irruptions of meaning that constitute the language of the spiritual world.

The invisible, by its nature, does not impose itself. It insinuates. And to perceive it, one must attune to a listening that goes beyond the physical senses. This attunement is what the ancients called *vis contemplativa*—the ability to contemplate, not with the eyes, but with the center of one's being. Developing this faculty requires time, patience, and an unarmed heart. The initiate must abandon the expectation of immediate results and learn to value discreet signs: an image that repeats in dreams, an emotion that suddenly rises during a prayer, a word heard by chance that answers an intimate question.

Over time, this listening becomes a permanent state. The operator begins to live in a state of ritual listening, even outside the ritual space. The boundary between rite and life begins to disappear. And it is at this moment that magic becomes real: when the invisible ceases to be an event and becomes a constant presence, a living pedagogy that instructs, corrects, and sustains.

12. Commitment to the Path

Preparation does not end after a ritual. It extends into life. An operator who performs the *Heptameron* becomes, in a way, a guardian of a path. This implies:

- Recording one's experiences: creating a detailed magical diary. Note not only what was done, but how one felt, what images arose, what internal resistances manifested. The diary is not a simple chronicle of ritual acts—it is a mirror of the inner journey. Over time, this record becomes a tool for self-knowledge and spiritual refinement. It allows the operator to recognize patterns, understand cycles, and perceive their own evolution with lucidity.
- Reflecting on the results with humility: the silence after the rite also communicates. Avoid anxiety for visible manifestations and learn to welcome what comes—or what does not come—with a spirit of listening. Sometimes, what does not happen is as significant as what does. The apparent void can be a time of invisible gestation, where deep forces reorganize before emerging into consciousness. The initiate must learn to

wait, not with passivity, but with attention and trust.
- Keeping the flame of the inner altar alive, with regular, even if simple, practices. Lighting a candle, reciting a psalm, entering into silence for a few minutes—each daily gesture is a brick that sustains the bridge between worlds. It is constancy that strengthens the channel. And the more the operator surrenders to this constancy, the more the invisible responds with presence. There is no need for constant grand rites: what is asked for is truth, continuity, and reverence.

It is this continuity that transforms a curious person into a true initiate. The curious seeks effects; the initiate seeks transformation. The curious wishes to control; the initiate wishes to serve. And it is this difference in posture that determines the degree of openness the invisible will grant. The path of the *Heptameron* is not a path of spectacles, but of consecration. And consecration is not an act, but a lifetime.

Preparation is not an isolated stage. It inaugurates a way of being. When the body is purified, the mind is silenced, and the spirit is oriented toward truth, a field is formed where the invisible can act with freedom. The circle, then, ceases to be just a drawing on the ground and becomes a real passageway. It is in this state of inner alignment that theophany becomes possible—not as a spectacle, but as a silent revelation.

The ladder of conjuration is made of gestures repeated with reverence, of words uttered with soul, of daily choices that consecrate the ordinary. And true magic, far from ready-made formulas, is this continuous commitment to wholeness. From the moment this commitment is made, every action is filled with meaning, every silence becomes fertile, and every ritual, a mirror of the sacred that pulses in the center of being.

Now, the external instruments can be fashioned. But let it not be forgotten: none of them will be effective if the operator has not, first, fashioned themself. For it is within the initiate that the true temple is erected—and it is there that the angels first respond.

Chapter 3
The Three Magic Circles

If inner preparation constitutes the operator's spiritual foundation, the drawing of the magic circles is the visible foundation upon which the entire rite will rest. In the *Heptameron*, the circle is not just a sacred boundary—it is a living mandala that organizes the invisible reality around the operator, creating a consecrated space-time where the worlds meet. This chapter is dedicated to the meticulous construction of the three magic circles: their proportions, symbolisms, sacred names, and exact layouts. Here, the practice begins to materialize.

Each line drawn on the ground is not mere ornamentation, but a key that opens portals between distinct spheres of being. The geometry of these circles, with their rigorous proportions and concentric layers, reflects an ordered worldview where chaos is contained and harmony is restored. The circle is not static—it is a living, pulsating organism that responds to the intention, devotion, and knowledge of the one who draws it. When the three circles are complete, intertwining the human, the angelic, and the elemental, a field of operation is formed where the ordinary laws of matter give way to the higher laws of the spirit.

The triple arrangement—inner, middle, and outer—mirrors the human being itself in its traditional division of spirit, soul, and body. Each circle fulfills a specific function, but all collaborate to establish a liminal reality, where ritual time imposes itself over chronological time. The operator, upon entering this space, is not merely protected: they are repositioned at the center of a magical cosmology that is structured around them. The inner circle is the altar of the heart; the middle circle, the celestial mind that calculates and orders; the outer circle, the boundaries and the guardians of the threshold.

The correct execution of the circles requires not only geometric precision but also full awareness of their symbolism. An error in inscription, an inversion of names, a displacement in the directions can compromise the integrity of the magical field, affecting its efficacy and safety. Therefore, the construction of the circles must be slow, deliberate, and meditative, like a prayer drawn with the body. The act of drawing itself becomes a rite, where each written name is a call, each line a symbolic seal, each symbol an anchor between the planes.

Furthermore, the materials used to draw the circles are not neutral. Chalk, flour, charcoal, or consecrated cloth function as symbolic supports with specific properties: chalk, for example, represents the element of air and is easily erased, making it suitable for ephemeral rites; flour, linked to earth and purity, evokes the sacredness of grains and spiritual nourishment; consecrated cloth, due to its durability, reflects the intention of continuity, serving as a symbolic reliquary of the portable temple. Choosing the right material is part of the magical act and must be done with discernment.

The positioning of the circles must also respect the energetic flows of the space. Ideally, the center of the inner circle should coincide with a point of silence and balance in the environment—an energetic nodal point, if possible. The alignment with the cardinal points, done with the aid of a compass, is not a mere technical whim: it reflects the ordering of the magical space with the cosmic directions and the archetypal forces that each direction represents. The east, for example, is the dawn and the beginning; the south, fire and action; the west, twilight and withdrawal; the north, mystery and introspection.

To draw the three circles is, therefore, much more than preparing the stage for a spiritual operation. It is to inscribe upon the physical world a living image of the hidden reality. It is to say, with silent acts: here, a temple is raised. Here, a passage is opened. Here, in the interweaving of sacred names, precise proportions, and pure intentions, magic becomes embodied. The operator, when walking upon this tracing, should feel not the weight of the ritual, but the lightness of being in harmony with the invisible order. For whoever understands the circle does not fear it—they revere it. And whoever draws it with righteousness, courage, and humility will see the invisible respond.

1. The Function of the Circle in Magical Tradition

Since the most ancient traditions, the circle has represented totality, unity, protection, and the sacred. It is the boundary that separates the profane from the consecrated. In the *Heptameron,* this structure is threefold—three concentric circles—and each layer fulfills a specific function. The circle is the body of the operator's portable temple. Within it, nothing can be done in a profane manner. It is a space where divine names circulate, celestial forces are organized, and the operator is elevated to a liturgical state.

More than a simple geometric shape, the circle is a spiritual reality condensed into a visible trace. In various ancient cultures—from Greece to the Semitic peoples, from the Celtic druids to the Egyptian priests—the circle appears as the primordial symbol of the ordered cosmos. It represents the womb of creation, the eye of the divine, the field where sacred transmutations are processed. When ritually drawn, the circle re-creates the world from its center, restoring the lost connection between the human plane and the higher spheres.

In the Western magical tradition, the circle is simultaneously protection and convocation. It protects the operator from influences that were not called and, at the same time, delimits the space where the invoked intelligences can manifest with safety and direction. Contrary to what some suppose, the circle does not serve merely to "contain" forces, but to organize them harmoniously. It is a vibrational matrix that regulates the entry and permanence of spiritual energies. Within this form, chaos is banished, and the higher order is established.

The triplicity of the circle in the *Heptameron* is not arbitrary. Each layer represents a degree of spiritual density, an instance of the celestial hierarchy, and a distinct mode of interaction with the sacred. The inner circle is the microcosm of the operator, where their soul aligns with the divine. The middle circle is the domain of celestial movement, where time, planets, angels, and astral rhythms are inscribed. The outer circle, in turn, is the symbolic wall that filters and directs the influxes of the elemental plane—especially the spirits of the air, messengers between worlds.

This concentric structure also reproduces the ancient concept of the ideal temple: a sacred nucleus, a ritual nave, and a liminal portico. Just as in the Hebrew tabernacle there was the Holy of Holies, the Holy Place, and the Courtyard, here too there are degrees of sanctity and distinct functions. To enter the first circle is like entering the heart of the temple—and each step beyond the threshold represents a change in inner state. The circle transforms ordinary space into sacred ground, and the operator into a priest of an invisible liturgy.

It is essential to understand that the circle does not possess power in itself. It is a receptacle, a form prepared to contain what the operator is capable of attracting through their intention, purity, and discipline. A circle drawn mechanically, without consciousness or reverence, is just a drawing on the floor. But a circle drawn with devotion, knowledge, and inner alignment becomes a field of real manifestation—a bridge between heaven and earth.

For this reason, many traditional texts insist that the operator never step inside the circle without preparation. This is not superstition, but respect for the subtle field established there. The circle is, so to speak, a mirror that reflects the operator's state. If they are centered, the circle will function as an instrument of elevation; if they are scattered or impure, the circle may reflect this disorder, attracting equally disordered forces.

Ultimately, the magic circle is a pedagogy of the sacred. It teaches, silently, that there is a time and a space for mystery. That there are boundaries that cannot be crossed with impunity. That the invisible requires form, and that form requires sacredness. The circle invites full presence, humility before the mystery, and a reunion with a greater order. Within its contours, the operator is not alone: they are in the company of ancestral intelligences, cosmic forces, and a truth that is not spoken, but lived.

2. Initial Practical Considerations

Before drawing the circles, the operator must ensure:

3. An appropriate environment: Choose a flat, clean, and quiet location where concentration can be maintained without risk of external interruptions. This space should be prepared beforehand, both physically and energetically, with ritual sweeping or smudging, if necessary.

4. Drawing materials: Procure white chalk, vegetable charcoal, consecrated flour, or a ritual wand

with a fine point. If a mobile and reusable support is preferred, use a plain white cloth of cotton or linen, which should be consecrated beforehand with appropriate prayers and incenses.

5. Precision instruments: Have a well-calibrated compass at hand, which will be used to accurately identify the cardinal points. It will also be necessary to have a long measuring tape or a string fixed to a central pin to draw the arcs with perfect symmetry. Small weights or stones can be used to maintain the stability of the cord while drawing.

6. Ritual references: Have the grimoire or the base text containing the sacred names, formulas, and seals to be used. The names should be clearly arranged in an organized sequence to avoid errors during inscription. The operator should familiarize themselves with each name before writing it, understanding at least minimally its meaning and spiritual function.

7. Operator's attire and state: It is recommended that the operator be dressed in a white or dark tunic (according to the tradition followed), of natural fabric and without secular symbols. The body should be purified by a ritual bath or appropriate abstinence. The state of mind should be serene, collected, and conscious of the seriousness of what will be performed.

8. Marking and drafting: Before making the final drawing, one can lightly mark the limits of each circle with small reference points, ensuring that all tracings will maintain the exact proportions. This is especially useful in outdoor environments, where the ground may have irregularities.

9. Appropriate time: The time chosen for the construction of the circles should be aligned with the purpose of the rite. For operations related to light, knowledge, or revelation, daylight hours are preferable. For introspective rites, of dissolution, or nocturnal invocation, crepuscular or nighttime hours are chosen. The choice of the moment should also consider the correspondence with the angels and rulers of the time, according to specific tables.

10. Opening the work: Before starting the tracing, it is recommended that the operator say a prayer of consecration for the space and a request for guidance from the higher beings. This opening establishes the first connection between the physical space and the spiritual plane.

Now, let us proceed to the description of each circle.

11. The Inner Circle: The Divine Presence

The inner circle is the most sacred. It is within it that the operator positions themself. It represents the core of the Divine Presence and is protected by sacred names and crosses. Its function is to protect the operator and anchor the invoked higher forces.

This first circle is the spiritual anchor of the rite, the silent heart of the invisible temple. Drawn with precision and reverence, it delimits the point where the operator's spirit unites with the divine principle. By positioning themself within this space, the operator symbolically dies to the outer world and is reborn in the sacred domain, becoming a conscious instrument of magical action.

- Instructions:
    1. Diameter: approximately 1.5 meters (about 5 feet). This size is sufficient for the operator to stand with arms extended to the sides without crossing the boundaries of the drawing.
    2. Inscription: In the four cardinal quadrants (East, South, West, North), four divine names should be written. A traditional example: ADONAI (East), ELOHIM (South), TETRAGRAMMATON (West), EL (North). The names should be written with clear and deliberate script, always starting from the East and proceeding clockwise.
    3. Central Cross: In the exact center of the circle, a cross with equal arms is drawn. On the horizontal axis, the word Alpha is written, and on the vertical axis, Omega—symbols of the beginning and the end, of the completeness of being in God.
    4. Symbol of Purity: Between each sacred name, a small cross is drawn, marking the limits between the names and reinforcing their protective function. These crosses function as subtle seals that energetically bind the four points and prevent psychic infiltration.

This circle should be drawn last, after the outer circles are complete, but consecrated first, as it is within it that the operator's axis will be established. Upon entering it, one must do so with a clear intention and a clean heart, mentally pronouncing a divine name or an opening prayer. No step within this circle should be taken carelessly, as it is, by its nature, the living altar of the operation.

12. The Middle Circle: The Wheel of Angels

The intermediate circle is the most complex and dynamic. In it are inscribed the names and sigils of the ruling angels of the hour, the day, the season, as well as celestial names associated with time and space. It is the circle of cosmic rhythm, where the cycles of the heavens are projected onto the earth and made present in the rite.

This circle is, in its essence, a living liturgical clock, a symbolic gear that translates the movements of the celestial bodies into sacred language. By inscribing the names of the angels and the rulers of time, the operator is not just recording information but activating a vibrational field that aligns the rite with the architecture of the cosmos. Precision in this inscription is essential to ensure the attunement between the terrestrial moment and the corresponding spiritual influxes.

- Instructions:
    1. Diameter: approximately 2.5 meters (about 8 feet). This size ensures that the circle comfortably surrounds the inner circle, creating a symbolic and vibrational space for angelic manifestation.
    2. Mandatory Inscription: a. The name of the current hour (e.g., Prime, Terce, None), according to the system of canonical hours.

b. The name of the Angel of the hour (consulted in specific tables, such as those in the *Heptameron*). c. The name of the Angel who governs the day of the week (e.g., Raphael for Wednesday). d. The names of the three ministers of that Angel, as indicated by the grimoire. e. The name of the current season of the year (Spring, Summer, Autumn, Winter). f. The names of the Spirits ruling the season and the presidents who command them. g. The head of the zodiacal sign ruling at that moment, according to the date and solar position. h. The traditional name of the Earth associated with the season (e.g., Auria, for Spring). i. The names of the Sun and the Moon, representing the luminary forces present in the current cycle.

These names should be inscribed in a harmonious order, distributed symmetrically around the circle, preferably in Latin or in sacred transliterations according to the textual source used. The most important thing is that the operator understands the meaning and function of each name—for it is this consciousness that gives life to the symbols.

This circle should be drawn with particular attention to the fluidity of the writing and the aesthetic arrangement, as it serves as a mirror of the firmament and a mechanism of celestial convocation. Light strokes can be used to pre-mark the inscription points, ensuring proportion and visual clarity. After completing it, a short prayer to the angels of time is recommended, asking that they guide and order the operation according to the laws of heaven. The Middle Circle is, in short, the axis where spiritual time meets the consecrated earth.

13. The Outer Circle: The Kingdom of the Spirits of the Air

This is the outermost circle, dedicated to the convocation and containment of the Intelligences of the Air—spirits that manifest in the four directions. They are the guardians of the threshold between worlds, agents of movement and subtle communication. In the *Heptameron*, each day of the week is under the regency of a specific set of spirits of the air, whose function is to mediate between the operator and the invisible planes with order and safety.

This circle functions as a vibrational shield, firmly delimiting the contours of the magical space. Its function is not only defensive but regulatory: by correctly naming the rulers of the air, the operator establishes a tacit pact of presence and cooperation. These spirits are summoned to witness, sustain, and balance the rite—never to dominate it. They keep the threshold inviolable, preventing uninvited energies from manifesting within the drawn temple.

- Instructions:
    1. Diameter: approximately 3.5 meters (about 11.5 feet). This measurement ensures that the outer circle surrounds the previous two with a wide margin, establishing a liminal zone between the profane world and the sacred world.

2. In the four cardinal corners (East, South, West, North), the operator must: a. Inscribe the names of the Presiding Spirits of the Air corresponding to the day of the operation, according to the *Heptameron*'s table. b. For each direction, write the name of a King of the Air (such as Oriens, Paimon, Amaymon, Egyn, etc.) and the names of three ministers associated with him. These names should be arranged clearly, with symmetry and respect for the cardinal positions.
3. Symbols: a. In each of the four cardinal angles, draw a pentagram with the point facing upwards. b. The points of the pentagrams must always be turned outwards from the circle, indicating celestial orientation and acting as swords of light that repel any adverse influence.

These pentagrams are not merely decorative: they condense within themselves the geometry of protection and the invocation of order. When drawing them, the operator must be in a state of full concentration, visualizing their symbolic function as beacons of stable energy.

- Recommendations for Inscription:
    1. Always work from the east in a clockwise direction, imitating the movement of the sun and following the rhythm of nature's manifestation.

2. Maintain a state of inner recollection and reverence throughout the entire execution. Each name should be inscribed with presence and, if possible, pronounced in a low voice or mentally while writing.
3. Avoid any form of distraction or conversation during the construction.
4. To deepen the sacredness of the moment, listen to psalms, Gregorian chants, or invocations in a low tone—sounds that elevate and stabilize the energetic field.
5. Upon finishing the inscription of the outer circle, recite a short sealing prayer, such as: "May this circle serve only light and truth, and may no spirit enter that has not been called in the name of the Most High."

This third circle should be the first to be physically drawn, as it defines the limits of the consecrated space. But it is the last to be spiritually activated, sealing the structure and summoning the watchers of the air. Once completed, the temple is enclosed—and the invisible awaits the call.

14. The Space Between the Circles

The space between the circles—especially between the inner and middle circles—is a zone of high vibrational sensitivity, where the mediation between the spiritual plane and the operator's consciousness occurs. It is not an empty space, but a symbolic transitional field where the spiritual presence projects itself with greater clarity. It is there that the angels, spirits, and intelligences summoned by the rite make their approach and, at times, their manifestation. Therefore, this space must be kept absolutely free and inviolate throughout the entire operation.

No profane object should be left in this interval. Nor should the operator or their assistants transit through it—neither before nor during the rite. The simple act of improperly crossing this zone can cause interference in the density of the field and hinder the condensation of the invoked presences. Ideally, the altar, when used, should be positioned within the inner circle or lightly touching its inner edge facing east, so that it never invades the space between the circles. The same applies to candles, censers, or any instruments: all must be anchored within the main sacred circle, never scattered across the threshold.

15. Temporary or Permanent Circle?

The choice between a temporary and a permanent circle depends on the nature of the magical work to be performed, as well as the frequency with which the operator practices. Temporary circles, drawn directly on the ground with chalk, charcoal, or consecrated flour, are especially useful for rites of a unique character, which require specific alignment with a particular moment, place, or intention. Their ephemerality is part of their strength: they are drawn with a clear purpose and undone after the work is finished, symbolically concluding the magical action.

On the other hand, the permanent circle is a ritual object in itself. Usually made of durable fabric, like cotton or linen, and painted with gold, silver, or white paint, it allows for multiple reuses and facilitates preparation in enclosed spaces. Before being used, it must be consecrated with lustral water, incense, and specific prayers, as it becomes a continuous receptacle of magical force. When not in use, it should be folded with reverence, wrapped in a clean cloth, and stored in a reserved place, away from vulgar energies. The permanent circle assumes, over time, the quality of a consecrated object, accumulating in its weave the vibrational memory of all rites performed.

Regardless of the model chosen, what gives power to the circle is the clear intention and proper consecration. A temporary circle drawn with reverence can be more effective than a neglected permanent one. What matters is not the durability of the form, but the clarity of the purpose that animates it.

16. The Importance of the Name

In the *Heptameron*—as in all theurgic-magical traditions—the name is a vehicle of presence. To name is to evoke; to write is to make manifest. Each sacred name, whether divine, angelic, or elemental, acts as a vibrational seal that connects the visible plane to the invisible. The name is not just a symbolic representation: it is the living signature of a spiritual intelligence.

During the inscription of names in the circles, the operator must keep their mind and heart united with what they are writing. One should not trace letters mechanically, but with full intention, pronouncing each name mentally (or softly in a low voice). This subtle vocalization, even if inaudible, serves as a vibrational catalyst, activating the presence of the designated spirit.

To write without attention is like knocking on a door and turning your back. To write with presence is to open a channel and remain receptive to what approaches.

This is why the names should not be copied carelessly. The operator must know them, understand their meaning, their origin, their function. By understanding the name, one becomes worthy of writing it. And by writing it with reverence, one becomes capable of summoning what it represents. This is the silent art of evocation. The name is the first step of manifestation. It is the initial vibration of the rite. It is the breath that awakens the invisible.

The operator who draws their circles is, in fact, architecting an invisible temple. Each drawn line is like a beam of light that supports an ethereal building, invisible to the eyes but tangible to the spirit. By inscribing a name, one is carving a seal into the subtle fabric of reality, opening a frequency that reverberates between the planes. The drawn symbols are not just ornaments: they are circuits of energy, points of contact between the manifest world and the higher spheres. Everything in this process—the gesture of the hand, the choice of direction, the cadence of the breath—composes a silent choreography of alignment between microcosm and macrocosm.

These three circles should not be understood as arbitrary borders, but as concentric orbits of a living liturgy. Each layer deepens the degree of consecration of the space. The first circle anchors the divine spark within the operator, establishing the altar of their presence. The second organizes celestial time and angelic influxes around the central axis. The third delimits the contours of the temple, filters access, and evokes the guardians of the threshold. Together, they create a vibrational chamber where the impossible becomes possible, where the rite ceases to be a metaphor and becomes an event.

Upon crossing the threshold of the first circle, the operator renounces the dispersion of the external world and assumes their priestly condition, becoming a bridge between worlds. Upon completing the third circle, the environment ceases to be a common place and becomes a consecrated territory, separated from ordinary time, attuned to the frequency of the rite. At that moment, the space is no longer just geographical—it is cosmological. And the operator is no longer an isolated individual, but a living center of convergence between the human and the divine.

This temple is not fixed; it has no walls or roof. But wherever the circles are drawn with righteousness, purity, and clear intention, there it will rise—invisible to the eyes, but perceptible to the spirit. For true magical architecture is not made of stone, but of intention, silence, and name. Within this temple, the operator does not invoke by force but invites with reverence. And that which responds to the call recognizes, in the precision of the line and the clarity of the gesture, the presence of someone who knows what they are doing. This is how the invisible manifests. This is how magic begins.

Chapter 4
The Operator's Tools

The magical rite described in the *Heptameron* is not merely an internal symbolic experience: it demands external preparation, specific instruments, and a visible commitment to the sacred. In this chapter, we will detail the tools necessary for the operator, both those that compose their altar and those that accompany their body. Each object described here is more than an accessory: it is a ritual extension of spiritual will. The correct preparation, consecration, and use of these tools are essential to ensure the integrity and effectiveness of the practice.

These instruments not only delimit the sacred space but also serve as anchors for magical consciousness, helping the operator maintain the required spiritual presence during the rite. The choice of each tool must be made with discernment and dedication, for they are more than physical utensils—they are living receptacles of the invoked energy. It is not uncommon for these objects, over time, to take on a presence of their own, becoming impregnated with the evoked forces and assuming an almost oracular role in the magician's life.

From the wood of the staff to the linen fiber of the robe, everything must be selected with intention. Natural materials are preferred, as they resonate more easily with the elemental principles. The act of personally crafting or adapting one's instruments, when possible, strengthens the bond between the operator and the invisible worlds. This material preparation is a devotional gesture that precedes the rite itself, marking a time of waiting, purification, and listening. It is a silent alchemical process, in which the operator themself becomes a tool. To handle each object with reverence—cleaning it, wrapping it, positioning it—is to already begin the rite, even before any word is spoken. No detail should be overlooked: the position of the candle, the order of the prayers, the texture of the fabric, the fragrance of the incense—everything communicates with the invisible.

These objects do not function in isolation; they form a symbolic orchestra where each element must be in harmony. When an instrument is out of place or poorly prepared, it can compromise the fluidity of the rite or attract unwanted influences.

Therefore, the magician must not only know the ritual properties of each item but also develop a living and continuous relationship with them, like one who cultivates a sacred garden. At the end of each work, it is not enough to simply put the instruments away: it is necessary to thank them, cleanse their energies, and return them to sacred rest. The constant maintenance of these bonds—through prayers, anointments, fumigations, and silences—transforms the ritual collection into a true spiritual body.

In this body, each tool is like a sensitive organ, connected to the breath of the spirit. In this way, the operator comes to inhabit not only the physical space of the rite but a subtle geography where everything becomes a sign. Cultivating this presence, this meticulous and loving care, is an essential part of the magical tradition preserved in the *Heptameron*.

- The Sacred Nature of the Tools

In ceremonial magic, every instrument is a point of contact between the visible and invisible worlds, a bridge that allows the operator to consciously transit between the dimensions of the rite. These objects have value not only for their physical form or beauty but for the role they play as vehicles of spiritual intention. When handled, they do not act on their own: they become conductors of consecrated will.

Each tool should be treated as a presence in itself, something living and receptive. There is a sacredness that emanates not from the object in its raw state, but from the bond established between it and the magician. That is why familiarization with each instrument should not be rushed. The operator needs to develop a refined sensitivity to its energy, understanding what it awakens in them and how it responds to various types of rituals. This mutual recognition between object and operator is what allows the full flourishing of its magical function.

When acquiring or crafting a tool, one should observe not only the material and form but also the moment and intention that permeate its origin. Items obtained in haste, carelessly, or out of ritual vanity tend not to integrate harmoniously into the practice. The ideal is for the instrument to be born from a process of listening and inner necessity, not from mere imitation or accumulation. It is preferable to have few tools, but ones imbued with meaning, than many devoid of soul.

The daily care of these objects—cleaning them, protecting them, anointing them, wrapping them in pure cloths—is part of the spiritual exercise itself. This is not superstition or preciousness, but respect for that which becomes a mirror of one's own soul at work. The instruments absorb and reflect the operator's internal states; they become extensions of their energy field. Therefore, they should not be handled by third parties, even well-intentioned ones, as they carry the unique mark of the bond with the one who consecrated them.

When not in use, the tools should rest in a reserved place, away from curious eyes and everyday banality. This consecrated space functions as a miniature sanctuary, where the energy of previous rites remains alive and latent. The mere presence of these objects in the environment already influences the spiritual atmosphere of the place, serving as a silent reminder of the operator's magical vocation.

It is also important to understand that the instruments do not possess autonomous power. They are not automatic talismans, but means. Their power is conditioned by the clarity, purity, and firmness of the will of the one who uses them. In unprepared hands, they become inert or, worse, points of energetic dissonance. But when treated with reverence and activated with a just intention, they operate as true keys between worlds.

Over time, the instruments may gain names, subtle responses, and even develop what some magicians describe as a "vibrational personality." This phenomenon, though mysterious, is a testament to the depth of the bond between operator and tool. In this sense, keeping a usage diary—where one records the reactions, sensations, and results obtained with each object—can be a valuable resource for deepening magical listening.

Therefore, even before the formal consecration, which will be treated in detail later, there is already an initiatory process underway: one that involves the care, listening, and dedication of the operator to their tools. To respect them is to respect one's own spiritual path. To recognize their sacredness is to recognize the sacredness of the office one embraces. And to honor their silence is to prepare the ground so that the Word of the rite may echo with truth.

- The Ritual Robe

The ritual robe is the first symbolic envelope of the separation between the everyday and the sacred. It represents, in its essence, purity, neutrality, and the consecration of the body to spiritual service. By putting it on, the operator not only prepares themselves externally but realigns their internal state with the priestly function they are about to perform.

- Color and material: Traditionally white, the tunic is made of cotton or linen, natural fabrics that do not retain subtle impurities and favor energetic circulation. The color white symbolizes not only light but also the transparency of intention and the cleanliness of the vibrational field, functioning as a mirror of the soul prepared for spiritual work.

- Style: It should be long, reaching the ankles, with long sleeves and without any kind of mundane adornment. When embroidered, a cross—if present—should be small and discreet, located on the chest or back, marking the subtle centers of the heart and spine as silent signs of orientation and surrender.
- Exclusive use: The tunic must not be worn outside the ritual space. After each rite, it should be carefully removed, folded with attention, and stored in a reserved place, away from profane eyes. Wrapping it in a white cloth protects its vibration. Before and after use, it is recommended to sprinkle it with holy water as a sign of respect for the role it fulfills.
- Consecration: Before being used for the first time, it must undergo a ritual consecration. This includes its fumigation with appropriate incense—such as frankincense or sandalwood—and the recitation of prayers dedicated to the divine light. This process not only purifies the fabric but invests it with a spiritual function that transcends its appearance.

Wearing this tunic is an act of passage. In doing so, the operator leaves behind their ordinary identities and assumes the sacred function of a mediator between

worlds. It is not a symbolic garment, but a true covering for the soul.
- The Wand or Ritual Staff

A symbol of spiritual authority and the direction of the will, the wand is one of the most important tools in the ceremonial arsenal. It not only represents the operator's power but acts as a direct extension of their ritual intention. It is with the wand that the limits of the sacred space are drawn, the circles of protection are traced, the forces are evoked, and the hidden formulas are imprinted upon the air.

- Material: Ideally made from natural wood—such as olive, oak, or walnut—the wand carries in its fiber the living memory of the plant element, its cycle, and its telluric force. The choice of wood should respect the resonance between its energy and the operator's intention. In some cases, copper may be used, a metal that symbolizes energetic conduction and communication between planes.
- Size: It is recommended that the wand be between 40 and 60 centimeters (16 to 24 inches) long, enough to be handled with precision without becoming an ostentatious object. Its length should correspond to the radius of action of the magician's will, so that the gesture that wields it contains both firmness and lightness.
- Form: Its tip can be carved with symbols that allude to the operator's spiritual work, or adorned with a sacred stone—such as amethyst, quartz, or obsidian—that serves as an energetic focus. The rest should be smooth, with a natural or lightly

polished texture, avoiding excesses that would disperse attention.
- Inscriptions: It is common to engrave divine names, personal seals, or the name of the ruling archangel of the day of the rite on its surface. These inscriptions should be made with reverence, at a propitious time, and never for decorative vanity. They are vibrational marks that amplify the wand's conductive power.
- Use: Its use is multiple—tracing the magic circle, blessing the elements of the altar, pointing in directions during invocations, channeling energy flows, and evoking specific presences. It acts as a bridge between the invisible and the conscious gesture.

It is with the wand that the operator "writes" the rite in space, as one who traces sacred calligraphy on the invisible fabric of the world. Each movement must be executed with clear intention, as the wand responds to the direction of the mind as much as to the firmness of the hand. To use it is to assume the responsibility of commanding the evoked forces. By raising it, the operator not only directs their will: they manifest the order they wish to establish in the ritual field.
- The Ritual Sword (optional)

The sword, although not explicitly prescribed in the *Heptameron*, appears as an extension of the wand in rites where the solemnity or intensity of the invocation requires a more imposing instrument. It does not replace the wand in its symbolic essence but amplifies it in rituals of direct command, complex banishments, or conjurations that deal with denser forces. Its use, therefore, demands spiritual maturity and mastery of the energetic field.

- Function: The main function of the sword is energetic delimitation. With it, the operator traces invisible boundaries in the ritual space, establishes circles of protection, and marks the cardinal points with greater intensity. It also acts as an instrument of command, through the symbolic force of the blade that cuts, separates, and orders. Furthermore, it is used in exorcisms and in practices that require a firm imposition of will over entities or subtle influences.
- Form: The ritual sword should be short and manageable, never a long weapon or one associated with profane combat. Its blade must be new or cleansed of any violent history; ideally, it should never have shed blood. The symbolism it carries is spiritual, not warlike. The hilt may contain protective inscriptions, such as tetragrams or seals of celestial authority, discreetly engraved.
- Use: The sword can be wielded with the operator's dominant hand, with precise and ceremonial movements. It is common for it to replace the wand when the rite requires strict containment of energies or the opening of deeper channels of manifestation. Its use requires absolute concentration, as it potentiates the magician's presence, projecting their will with clarity and force.

The sword demands greater mental discipline precisely for this reason: it does not tolerate distraction. Every gesture made with it reverberates with more intensity in the subtle field. It is a tool that imposes clarity, exactness, and focus. Its presence on the altar is a sign of a more elevated rite or an operation that requires greater spiritual responsibility. The one who wields it must know what they seek, why they call, and how far they are willing to go.

- The Censer or Clay Vessel

Used to burn perfumes and incenses during rituals, the censer represents the point of symbolic combustion between the physical and spiritual worlds. It is in the censer that the consecrated fire becomes the bearer of prayer, elevating it in the form of smoke to the subtle planes. Its presence on the altar is not decorative but functional and profoundly symbolic.

- Material: The most traditional is a new clay vessel, for its simplicity and connection to the Earth element. However, heat-resistant metal containers are also acceptable, especially when used with reverence and proper preparation. The important thing is that they have never been used for profane purposes.
- Form: It should be simple, with a top opening to accommodate the charcoal and a firm base that ensures stability during use. The absence of adornments or reliefs facilitates cleaning and avoids visual distractions during the rite.
- Use: Upon the burning charcoal—previously exorcised—the perfume or incense corresponding

to the day or the invoked archangel is placed. The operator should do this with clear intention, usually accompanying the gesture with a silent prayer or invocation. The rising smoke is not just fragrance: it is presence, vehicle, and response.

- Symbolism: The censer synthesizes two elements—fire and air—in a single ritual manifestation. The fire, tamed and sanctified, represents the transmuting force and the ardor of the spiritual will. The air, through the smoke, expresses the sacred breath, the spirit in motion, the prayer that ascends.

The preparation of the censer must be done with attention and respect. The choice of charcoal, the purity of the incense, and the way the flame is lit directly influence the vibrational quality of the ceremony. The act of censing—whether the altar, the tools, or the operator themself—establishes a vertical axis between the visible and the invisible, between Earth and Heaven.

Even when not in ritual use, the censer should be kept clean, free of residues, and stored with the other sacred instruments. It is, par excellence, a conductor of ardent prayer—and its silence, when at rest, still holds the echo of the invocations it has conducted.

- Perfumes and Incenses

Each day of the week has its own perfumes, aligned with the vibrational nature of the ruling archangel. The choice of the appropriate scent is not just a symbolic deference but a vibrational key that attunes the space to the spiritual influx of that specific day. The incense acts as an invisible vehicle for prayer, elevating requests, purifying the environment, and strengthening the invoked presence.

- Sunday (Michael): frankincense, benzoin. Scents that evoke solar strength, clarity of spirit, and ardent protection.
- Monday (Gabriel): myrrh, amber. Lunar perfumes that open the channels of intuition and welcome messages from the unconscious.
- Tuesday (Samael): sulfur, rue. Strong substances for rituals of intense purification and combating adverse influences.
- Wednesday (Raphael): sandalwood, lavender. Healing, calming essences conducive to angelic communication.
- Thursday (Sachiel): cinnamon, bay laurel. Warm and expansive notes that favor prosperity, justice, and balance.
- Friday (Anael): rose, jasmine. Venusian perfumes that awaken beauty, harmony, and affective openness.
- Saturday (Cassiel): cypress, black amber. Dense, introspective scents, geared towards meditation, containment, and contact with the occult.

These perfumes should be burned on consecrated charcoal in the censer, beginning the ritual process with reverence and silence. The operator should, whenever possible, make a conscious choice of incense before the rite, attuning their mind to the archangel of the day. By observing the reactions of the environment—the density of the smoke, its direction, the persistence of the aroma—the magician can also perceive subtle signs from the invisible plane.

The correct use of perfumes not only harmonizes the energy field but also defines the spiritual frequency of the operation. In certain cases, the combination of scents can be adjusted for more complex rites, as long as the operator is attentive to the symbolic compatibility of the elements. To burn the appropriate perfume is to speak the language of the spirits, offering them an olfactory path to make themselves present.

- Lustral Water (Holy Water)

Used to purify the circles, the instruments, and the operator themself, lustral water is the liquid sacrament of ceremonial magic. Before any invocation or ritual tracing, it seals the space, dissolves subtle residues, and makes the spiritual ground of the practice fertile. Its preparation requires clear intention and respect for tradition.

- Preparation: Lustral water is obtained from the union of two fundamental elements—pure water and previously consecrated salt. This joining should be done in a state of recollection, with the container facing east or north, according to the tradition followed. While pouring the salt into the water, the operator can chant Psalm 51, known as "Miserere mei, Deus," asking for the purification of the spirit and the cleansing of the space. The prayer should be done with concentration and humility, visualizing the infusion of light into the substance. The resulting water is not just a physical mixture but a vehicle of spiritual power.

- Use: With a sprig of hyssop, boxwood, or with one's own fingers, the lustral water is sprinkled around the magic circle, over the altar, instruments, and over the operator's own body. The gesture should be slow, measured, and mentally accompanied by an appeal to the divine presence. By touching the cardinal points, the operator reinforces the invocation of the spiritual guardians of the space. The use of the water should occur before any other ritual action, as it dissolves psychic miasmas, deprograms residual energies, and establishes a new field of spiritual action.
- Symbolism: Lustral water represents the baptism of matter by light. It carries the power to transmute the profane space into a sacred enclosure, making the magical operation possible with safety and clarity. Its use is not only practical but symbolic: each sprinkled drop affirms the operator's spiritual authority and invisibly delimits the boundary between the ordinary world and the territory of the rite.

Lustral water, when well-prepared and applied with reverence, becomes a luminous shield against external interference and a catalyst for the manifestation of sacred designs. The simple act of touching it, feeling its temperature, its light scent (when perfumed with consecrated herbs), already repositions the spirit on the axis of the sacred. Stored in an appropriate vial, protected from direct sunlight, and accessed only in ritual contexts, this water remains alive and operative for long periods.

- Consecrated Salt

An instrument of protection and vibrational stabilization, consecrated salt is one of the oldest elements of magical practice. Considered a symbol of incorruptibility and preservation, it acts as a spiritual barrier against chaotic forces and as an anchor for the ordering of the sacred space.

- Use: Small mounds of consecrated salt can be placed in the four corners of the ritual circle, at the cardinal points, functioning as vibrational sentinels. A continuous line can also be traced with it, forming a perimeter of containment around the altar or the operator. When necessary, a handful can be thrown into the fire, water, or other elements to reinforce their stability.
- Consecration: The salt must be exorcised before use, through prayer and the laying on of hands. A traditional formula consists of tracing a cross over it, saying: "I exorcise thee, creature of salt, by the light of the living God, that thou mayest become salt of wisdom and shield of truth, driving away all evil and sealing this place in the name of the Light." Afterward, the operator can breathe upon the salt or raise it to the heavens, symbolically offering it to the higher forces.
- Symbolism: Salt represents the fixation of spiritual intention on the material plane. It not only protects but stabilizes. Its power lies not in its chemical composition but in the symbolic

charge it carries when ritually activated. The presence of consecrated salt in the magical space establishes an axis of order and resistance to spiritual dissolutions.

At the end of the rite, the salt that was used should be discarded on virgin soil or dissolved in running water, never reused. This practice ensures that it has fully fulfilled its function and that there is no accumulation of energetic residues for the next work. To handle it with respect is to recognize its role as an invisible guardian of magical balance.

- The Ritual Candle or Lamp

The presence of light is indispensable in every magical rite based on the *Heptameron*. It not only illuminates the physical space but activates the spiritual dimension of the altar, serving as a beacon that attracts, orders, and sustains the manifestation of the invoked presences.

- Color: The candle should be white, as a universal symbol of purity and neutrality, or, preferably, of the color corresponding to the ruling planet of the day of the rite—for example, gold for the Sun (Sunday), silver for the Moon (Monday), red for Mars (Tuesday), green for Mercury (Wednesday), blue or purple for Jupiter (Thursday), pink for Venus (Friday), and black or violet for Saturn (Saturday). This correspondence reinforces the vibrational attunement of the work.
- Position: The main candle should occupy the center of the altar or be placed directly in front of the operator, marking the axis of their intention.

In more elaborate rites, other candles may be placed at the cardinal points or around the circle, as long as they are aligned with the harmony of the operation.
- Symbolism: The flame represents the divine spark, the living spirit, the clarity of the mind, and the active presence of the will. It not only illuminates but consecrates. The fire of the candle is the visible manifestation of the invisible light. Its silent dance upon the altar is read as a subtle response to the invoked forces.

The candle should be lit with an inner or verbalized prayer, invoking the light of God or the ruling archangel of the day. Its flame should never be blown out: it is extinguished with the fingers or with a proper snuffer, always with reverence, giving thanks for the light granted. The wick and the remains of the candle should be treated with respect—never thrown in the common trash, but buried or cast into a current, in a rite of return.

- The Grimoire

More than a book, the grimoire is a living tool of contact with the spiritual tradition. In the context of the *Heptameron*, it must always be present in the ritual space, functioning as a guide, a witness, and a mirror of the operation.
- Form: It can be printed or handwritten, as long as it maintains the integrity of the original texts and seals. Many magicians prefer to copy the most used passages by hand, as the act of writing

already begins the process of connecting with the contents.
- Treatment: The grimoire should never touch the ground directly. It should rest on a white cloth, preferably consecrated, or on a dedicated ritual table. It should be kept in a clean place, away from profane hands, and covered when not in use.
- Use: During the rite, the operator consults it to chant prayers, evocations, invocations, formulas, and to verify the names and seals of the spirits. The simple act of opening it is a magical gesture, which must be done with full attention.

To treat the grimoire with devotion is to recognize that it contains, within itself, a condensation of ancestral wisdom. It is the map and also the sanctuary. To handle it is like touching an invisible thread that connects the magician to previous generations of seekers of the hidden light. The grimoire is more than instruction: it is presence.

- Other Complementary Elements

In addition to the main instruments, certain complementary elements can be incorporated into the rite to strengthen the stability of the energy field and favor the operator's spiritual concentration. Although they are not formal requirements, their well-oriented presence can amplify the effectiveness of the operation and offer additional layers of protection, anchoring, and direction.

- Anchoring crystals: The use of crystals such as white quartz, amethyst, or obsidian serves to consolidate the energetic presence of the ritual space. White quartz, for its neutrality and power of amplification, harmonizes and stabilizes the environment. Amethyst, with its higher frequency, favors spiritual opening, protecting against astral disturbances. Obsidian, being denser, creates a firm barrier against external interference. These crystals should be strategically positioned, such as at the four corners of the altar or at the operator's feet, and periodically purified under moonlight or with appropriate smudging.

- Ritual cloth: A white cloth, of linen or cotton, can be used to cover the altar or wrap the instruments when not in use. This cloth acts as a membrane of spiritual silence, isolating the ritual field from profane interference and helping to preserve the consecrated vibration of the objects. At the end of each operation, it should be folded carefully and stored separately from other common fabrics, and it can also be sprinkled with lustral water or censed before each use.

- Bell or chime: The metallic sound of the ritual bell is used to demarcate thresholds between phases of the rite, such as the opening and closing, or to attract the attention of spiritual presences. Its tone should be clear, sharp, and brief, so as to pierce the subtle layers of the space and symbolically order the planes. Ringing the bell is not a mere announcement: it is a ritual gesture of convocation. The operator must handle it with precise intention, respecting the silence that follows its echo as a space for spiritual reception.

These items, although not mandatory, when integrated with wisdom and discretion, offer additional support to the structure of the rite. The decision to include them should come from inner listening and an understanding of the specific demands of each operation. An excess of elements without a clear purpose can disperse focus. But when each addition is the result of a true need, the rite flourishes in its harmonic complexity.

- Care of the Tools

The maintenance of ritualistic tools is a fundamental part of magical discipline. Just as the body must be purified before the rite, the instruments also require constant attention, as they are extensions of the operator's intention and silent guardians of the bond with the invisible.

- They should be stored in a clean place, away from the curious: The space where they rest should be reserved exclusively for spiritual practice, without the circulation of uninitiated people. It can be a consecrated drawer, a wooden chest, or a cabinet that functions as a small domestic sanctuary. The energy of the place directly interferes with the vibrational quality of the instruments.
- They should never be lent, sold, or profaned: A magical tool carries the psychic and spiritual impressions of the magician who consecrated it. When touched by third parties, even without ill intent, it can lose its attunement or be

contaminated by foreign fields. Selling them or using them for profane purposes breaks their spiritual bond and distorts their function.

- They can be ritually re-consecrated if they are broken or violated: If a tool breaks, is lost, or profaned, the operator must carefully assess whether the bond can still be restored. In some cases, a rite of reconnection can be performed, involving intense purification, re-consecration, and symbolic fasting. In others, it will be necessary to prepare a new instrument from scratch, with due mourning for the previous one.
- They should be regularly purified with incense and prayer: Even when not in use, the tools accumulate resonances from the environment and require periodic cleansing. Fumigation with frankincense, myrrh, or sandalwood, accompanied by prayer, restores their vibrational clarity. It is also possible to use lustral water or leave them under the light of the full moon, depending on the type of instrument and the tradition followed.

To care for the tools is to care for the continuity of the path. The operator who takes good care of their instruments cares, ultimately, for their own fidelity to the spiritual path they have chosen. These objects, silent but attentive, guard the echoes of the sacred words already spoken and prepare the invisible space for those yet to come.

When the operator understands that each tool is not just a means, but a silent witness to the sacred, their relationship with the rite is radically transformed. The dedication offered to these instruments—from their origin to their use and rest—reflects the degree of alignment between intention and action, between the invisible that is sought and the visible that is manifested. In each gesture of care, in each moment of silence beside a lit candle or before a closed grimoire, the pact between the human and the spiritual world is renewed. To cultivate this presence is to recognize that the rite begins long before the first word is uttered and continues to vibrate long after the last candle has gone out.

Chapter 5
Blessing of the Circle

In the rite of the *Heptameron*, the creation of the magic circle is only the beginning of a much deeper process: its consecration. The circle, once drawn, is not yet spiritually active. It is, at that moment, merely a geometric form in space. What makes it sacred, vibrant, and capable of containing and channeling spiritual intelligences is the blessing. In this chapter, we will learn how to transform a structure traced with chalk, charcoal, or cloth into a living space of spiritual manifestation.

When traced, the circle symbolically delimits the boundary between worlds. But this line, by itself, is mute. It needs to be awakened, animated by a gesture that makes it permeable to spiritual presence. The blessing is that gesture—and not just one, but a linked sequence of actions aimed at turning geometry into a living channel of grace. Blessing, in this sense, is not a liturgical adornment, but a conscious invocation that transforms matter into sacrament.

Before being a space of manifestation, the circle is a mirror of the operator's soul. It reflects their inner disposition, their order, their clarity of intention. By blessing it, the magician also blesses themselves, reaffirms their surrender to the path of light, and reminds themself that the sacred begins in the simplest gesture. That is why each step of the blessing rite must be done with sacred slowness, loving attention, and true reverence.

The blessing is a spiritual work of art in miniature: it begins in the word, passes through the water, ascends in the smoke, and is established in the gesture. Therefore, one must never rush it or perform it mechanically. Each syllable spoken, each drop sprinkled, each spark of incense lit, each cross traced in the air must be full of presence. For it is thus that the invisible responds: to presence.

And when this presence is authentic, the circle responds. It becomes silent, it pulsates, it delimits. It becomes a womb and a temple, a shield and an altar. The blessing, then, ceases to be an act of the operator and becomes an event between worlds. The line drawn on the ground becomes the contour of a more subtle reality, where only that which is true may enter.

- The Spiritual Meaning of the Blessing

The word "blessing," derived from the Latin *benedictio*, carries within it the primary meaning of "to say well," that is, to utter words charged with creative potency. In the context of ceremonial magic, this expression goes beyond its usual devotional use. The blessing of the circle is an act that imprints a new identity upon the delimited space: it removes it from the ordinary plane and inscribes it into the geography of the sacred. The circle, upon being blessed, ceases to be a geometric line and becomes an inviolable territory, a point of contact between the worlds.

To say well, in this rite, is to speak with precision, with purity of intention, and in consonance with the divine will. The operator, by pronouncing words of blessing, becomes not the author, but the channel of the higher order. They name not according to their own will, but as one who echoes an already existing spiritual truth. The blessing, therefore, is a recognition: the space is not taken by force, but offered, sanctified by presence and word.

More than protecting, the blessing clarifies. It establishes an atmosphere of spiritual lucidity within the circle, creating a vibrational clearing where consciousness can expand without interference. The magician, by executing this rite, makes a pact of light. The blessed line is a symbolic and operative boundary: everything within it submits to the invoked order; everything outside is kept at a distance by the integrity of the intention.

The blessing of the circle is also a gesture of humility: the operator recognizes that it is not they who hold the power, but that they act as a servant of a greater order. The gesture of blessing is not one of imposition, but of listening. That is why it is common for many magicians, upon completing the rite of consecration, to experience a sensation of lightness or expanded presence—as if the space now breathes in unison with a higher reality.

Finally, the blessing consecrates not only the space but also time. From that moment on, the time within the circle begins to obey another cadence—that of the rite. It is a spiraling, symbolic time, oriented by gestures and words that hallow it. The operator, upon entering the blessed circle, enters a different rhythm: they leave profane time and inscribe themself in ritual eternity.

Therefore, the blessing of the circle is simultaneously foundation and offering, shield and invocation, silence and word. It affirms: "here, the sacred has a place." And this affirmation, when made with truth, is heard.

- The Four Elements in the Blessing

The blessing of the circle is an invocation that operates through the harmonization of the four fundamental elements: water, fire, air, and earth. Each one participates as a symbolic and energetic vector that awakens, balances, and consecrates the delimited space. They are not used as mere props, but as archetypal forces that, when correctly mobilized, establish the spiritual presence.

- Water (lustral water): Represents the principle of purification. By sprinkling the circle with lustral water, the operator dissolves the subtle impurities that may be present in the field. This gesture symbolizes a baptism of the space, preparing it to receive the light. Water is the liquid memory of the sacred and, upon touching the earth, re-consecrates it as an altar.
- Fire (incense or light): Through the flame that consumes the incense or the light of the ritual candle, fire is introduced as a transmuting element. It consumes the dense, elevates the prayer, and makes the invisible visible through

the rising smoke. More than purifying, fire consecrates. Its heat awakens, its light clarifies, its flame seals the pact with the heavens.
- Air (the word, breath): The air enters through the spoken word, the conscious breath, the prayers and invocations that echo during the rite. It carries the intention, transmits the will, and makes the space vibrate with the frequency of the invoked presence. The word, articulated with purity, acts as a subtle sword that traces boundaries between the profane and the sacred.
- Earth (the traced circle itself): The earth is the foundation. The circle, as a geometric form on the ground, anchors the spiritual energies in a specific place. It is the receptacle that welcomes and sustains. Its tracing establishes the alliance between the above and the below, offering the light a point of grounding. It is on the earth that the other elements act and integrate.

When these four elements are brought together in the rite of blessing, a field of harmony is created that mirrors the cosmic order. They do not act in isolation, but in mutual resonance. Water and fire purify and consecrate; air and earth transmit and sustain. Together, they build a sacred matrix where the spiritual can manifest with safety and truth. In this space, the circle does not just protect: it calls. It does not just delimit: it reveals. And the presence, then, responds.
- Necessary Materials

To perform the blessing of the circle properly and effectively, it is essential for the operator to have the necessary instruments, each with its precise function in the ritual sequence. These items are not just physical tools: they are conductors of intention, channels of spiritual action. Their presence must be organized in advance, and their placement around the circle thought of as part of the rite.

- Lustral water: Should be prepared beforehand with pure water and consecrated salt, both exorcised by a specific prayer. This water is used to sprinkle the circle and represents the initial purification of the space, dissolving any energetic residue that still connects it to the ordinary plane. Water, in this context, is a link between the body of the rite and the subtle dimension of the blessing.
- Consecrated sprig: This can be hyssop, rosemary, rue, or another ritually appropriate herb, preferably fresh. This sprig is used as an instrument of aspersion, imbuing it with purifying intention. Each leaf becomes, at that moment, an emissary of the grace one wishes to summon.
- Incense of the day: Chosen according to the planetary correspondence of the week, the incense establishes the vibrational perfume that attunes the space to the desired angelic sphere. It should be natural, preferably in grains, resins, or specific blends, and not replaced with artificial versions.
- Censer with burning charcoal: The vessel holding the charcoal must be heat-resistant and safe to handle while moving. The charcoal needs to be lit before the rite begins, allowing the incense to

produce a continuous and dense smoke during the fumigation of the circle. The smoke should circulate like a veil between the worlds.
- Wand or ritual staff: A symbol of magical authority, the wand is the extension of the operator's will. With it, signs and crosses are traced during the consecration. It must be previously consecrated and only used in ritual contexts, being handled with respect and clarity of intention.
- Grimoire: The book of prayers and guidance should be open to the specific text of the blessing, accessible to the operator without the need for movement or distraction. It is not just a manual but a spiritual anchor of the tradition being embodied in the rite.
- Ritual robe: Must be worn from the beginning, symbolizing the shedding of profane garments and the entry into the priestly function. It should be clean, purified, and, if possible, previously sprinkled with lustral water. Its presence reinforces the threshold between the common and the sacred.

Each of these items should be arranged in advance on the altar or near the circle, in an intuitive and practical order. The operator should not improvise during the rite: every movement should flow naturally from the silent and careful preparation that precedes it. Thus, the rite of blessing becomes, from the very first gesture, an expression of the order it invokes.

- The Rite of the Blessing of the Circle

Below is the traditional sequence for the blessing of the circle, adapted for the modern operator. It is recommended that the rite take place with the operator already dressed in the tunic, in a state of inner silence. The prior preparation is as essential as the execution: before beginning, the operator must ensure that all elements are positioned, the environment is silent, and their mind is collected. The tunic, a symbol of the spiritual office, should envelop the body like a ritual skin, separating the profane self from the priestly presence manifesting there.

- 1. Silence and Reverence

Begin with a posture of prayer. Standing outside the yet-unconsecrated circle, the operator breathes deeply, quiets their thoughts, and establishes their inner intention:

"I consecrate this circle to the divine light. May no shadow profane this space. May only the forces of truth, wisdom, and peace dwell here."

This moment is more than a formal introduction: it is a threshold. The invoked silence is not the absence of sound, but an expanded presence. The quietude is not passivity, but listening. By silencing themselves, the operator becomes a receptacle for the higher intention, allowing their physical, emotional, and mental presence to align with the sacred gesture about to be initiated. This initial reverence is a sign that everything within the rite will be done not by automatism, but by full consciousness.

- 2. Asperges Me Domine

With the lustral water in a bowl and the sprig of hyssop or rosemary, the operator slowly walks around the circle in a clockwise direction, sprinkling drops of water on the lines of the circle while reciting in a solemn voice:

"Asperges me, Domine, hyssopo et mundabor: lavabis me, et super nivem dealbabor."

Translation: "You will sprinkle me with hyssop, Lord, and I shall be purified; You will wash me, and I shall be made whiter than snow."

This phrase comes from Psalm 51, traditionally used in rites of purification. While walking, the operator visualizes the water cleansing any previous energetic residue.

This initial purification is a gesture of humility and clarification of the field. The operator does not walk out of formality, but as one reopening an ancient sacred path. The water, consecrated and exorcised, becomes a conductor of spiritual light. The sprig, in turn, is not a mere utensil: it is a vegetal emissary of intention, a channel of living blessing. Each drop cast upon the ground of the circle is a seed of purity. The operator can imagine the water expanding into luminous filaments beneath the traced line, like subtle roots that dissolve shadows and densities.

The rhythm of the walk should follow the breath. There is no rush. Each step can be inwardly accompanied by a silent prayer, reinforcing the link between gesture and consciousness. Visualizing the water washing not only the floor but also the subtle layers of the space—as if cleaning invisible veils between worlds—intensifies the consecratory effect. The circle, little by little, ceases to be a drawing on the floor and begins to behave like a field. Some magicians report that, upon performing this step with true presence, they experience a sudden change in the density of the air, a pause in ordinary time, as if the space were breathing with a new cadence.

Upon completing the circuit, the operator may pause for a brief moment, raising the sprig over the center of the circle and tracing a cross in the air with it. This gesture, though simple, symbolically seals the purification stage and prepares the transition to the vibrational elevation that will be performed by the fire of the incense. The water has opened the way. The circle is now prepared to become an altar.

- 3. Fumigation of the Circle

After the aspersion, the operator lights the incense corresponding to the day and places it on the charcoal in the censer. They walk again around the circle, letting the smoke envelop the entire traced perimeter. This walk should be slow, deliberate, almost ceremonial, as if each step were being taken upon a veil between worlds. The movement of the smoke, in ascending spirals, is not just physical—it carries, in its invisible wake, the intention of elevation, of superior purification, and of the definitive consecration of the space.

While walking, the operator may recite in a low but firm and measured voice:

"Let my prayer rise like incense before You, Lord. And may this circle be as the altar where Your presence manifests."

This phrase, inspired by Psalm 141, summarizes the intention of this stage: to make the environment become an altar, to make the prayer become a bridge. The smoke, in this context, is more than a byproduct of combustion: it is the concrete visualization of the prayer ascending, of matter becoming spirit, of the invisible taking form. Many magicians report that, at this moment, the air acquires a different thickness, as if the space were being gently sealed by layers of subtle presence.

The operator should allow the smoke to touch every point of the circle, not just as a mark of passage, but as an aerial anointing. It can be guided with the free hand, or with a ritual gesture using the wand, so as to direct its ascent. The important thing is that this smoke travels along the entire line drawn on the ground, as if writing the secret name of the space with perfume. The fumigation completes the work of the water: where before there was dissolution, now there is consecration and elevation.

During the circuit, the magician can visualize the circle being enveloped by a luminous film, as if the smoke were activating a membrane between the planes, transforming the physical perimeter into a vibrational boundary. With each step, the intention is reinforced: may the fire consecrate, may the smoke elevate, may the air respond. This is the moment when the circle begins to emit a specific kind of silence: the one that precedes manifestation. It is common that, at the end of the fumigation, the operator feels that time has slowed down and the air has gained density and clarity. There is, at times, a feeling of light static electricity, as if the space has been awakened.

Upon completing the circuit, the censer can be placed with reverence on the altar or on a stone on the ground, allowing the smoke to continue rising throughout the following stages. The fire remains, discrete but vigilant, keeping the bridge between worlds alive. The circle, now purified by water and elevated by fire and air, is ready to receive the seals of the word. The next step will be the verbal and directional consecration with the ritual wand, sealing the four cardinal points and the center as vertices of the sacred.

- Post-Blessing: Signs of Activation

After the rite of blessing, the operator may feel subtle changes in the environment—silent, yet unmistakable, signs that the spiritual field has been effectively awakened. One of the most recurrent manifestations is a sudden sensation of lightness in the air, as if the internal gravity of the space had decreased. On other occasions, the opposite occurs: a palpable density, almost like an invisible veil enveloping the body, which does not oppress but protects. This ambivalence is a sign that the threshold between planes has been successfully crossed.

The silence also thickens. Not just the absence of external sounds, but a kind of sonic recollection in which even the breath seems to partake in a deeper quietude. It is common that, in this state, thoughts slow down, emotions become peaceful, and time seems suspended. The operator feels themselves within a distinct vibrational interval, where each gesture acquires an amplified symbolic weight. The mind clears, not through effort, but through resonance with the invoked order.

Another notable sign is the clear perception of the circle's boundary. Even without looking at the ground, the operator distinctly feels the limits of the consecrated space, as if an energetic membrane had been stretched around it. This sensation of delimitation is not merely intuitive: for many, it presents as a sudden change in air temperature upon approaching the edge, or as a subtle resistance when trying to cross it without conscious intention.

This activation can also provoke a state of expanded attention, in which the senses seem more awake and mental focus intensifies. The gaze becomes deeper, hearing more acute, and intuition more present. It is as if the vibrational field is now modulating perception, aligning it with the purpose of the rite. For the sensitive operator, this state may even manifest as a tactile perception of spiritual presences—not as figures, but as subtle intelligences that begin to circulate within the sacred sphere.

Therefore, once the field is activated, it is fundamental that the operator remains within the circle until the complete end of the operation. Leaving the consecrated perimeter before ritually closing it can break the integrity of the space and prematurely dissolve the constructed vibrational weave. To remain within is to respect the established sacredness, to inhabit the temple with full consciousness.

- Renewals and Repetitions

The blessing of the circle is not an isolated act, but a continuous commitment. Whenever the circle is erased, moved, or drawn in a new location, it must be blessed again, as its link to the spiritual order is inseparable from the space and time in which it was traced. Even permanent circles—on cloth, tarps, or fixed structures—require ritual renewal for each operation. The sacred is not a static structure: it is a state that needs to be constantly summoned and nurtured.

In prolonged rituals that extend over more than one day, it is recommended that the blessing be reinforced at each new session. This can be done by burning new incense, a brief prayer of reconnection, and, if necessary, a new tracing with the wand. The repetition of the blessing is not redundancy: it is a reaffirmation of the vow, a reopening of listening, a maintenance of the alliance.

Just as a flame needs to be fed to not go out, the consecrated field of the circle needs to be kept vibrant by the conscious renewal of the bond. Each time the blessing is repeated with truth, the space responds. It does not just become functional—it becomes habitable for the spirit.

- Circle and Ethics

By consecrating the circle, the operator not only delimits a ritual space but silently affirms their adherence to a code of spiritual conduct. Every line drawn on the ground, every word spoken, every gesture executed within this perimeter now operates under an implicit ethic: that no action performed there can contradict the principles that found the light. The circle, once blessed, becomes not just a magical tool but a temple—and every temple demands reverence, coherence, and responsibility.

This means that the operator, upon crossing the consecrated boundary, commits not to their personal desires, but to the truth that was invoked there. The blessing, in this context, is more than an authorization to act: it is an inner vow of integrity. No enchantment, no invocation, no petition should be made within the circle if it is not aligned with the principles of truth, love, and wisdom. Any deviation from this triad makes the act not only ineffective but spiritually dangerous, as it breaks the alliance sealed in the rite.

The ethics of the circle also demand constant vigilance over one's motivations. The magician is invited to examine, before any operation, whether their intention springs from a luminous center or from egoic impulses disguised as a spiritual quest. The consecration of the circle does not only purify the space: it illuminates intentions. And everything that cannot withstand this light must be left outside. That is why many operators say a prayer of humility or make a silent confession before crossing the sacred line: not out of superstition, but out of honesty.

Operations performed in unconsecrated circles—or circles consecrated superficially, hastily, without presence—become unstable, fragmented, and sometimes even energetically corrosive. The absence of a blessing does not mean neutrality: it means exposure. It means the operator is navigating a deep symbolic territory without the safeguards the rite should provide. Therefore, one must never begin any practice without the gesture of blessing. It is not an optional detail: it is the foundation.

Blessing and ethics, therefore, are inseparable. The blessing seals the intention, and the intention, in turn, must be sustained by a life that supports it. The circle becomes an altar not because it was drawn, but because it is inhabited with consciousness. And this consciousness must endure even after the rite ends, like a spark that continues to shine in the operator's daily life. To act outside the circle with the same truth with which one acts within it—this is the true purpose of the practice.

With each new tracing, with each new blessing, the operator is reminded: spiritual power is not a right, it is a concession. And this concession only remains alive to the extent that it is treated with respect, devotion, and inner righteousness. Thus, the circle ceases to be just a technique and becomes a path. A path where every step, however silent, is heard. Where every gesture, however small, is recorded. And where the divine presence, once called with truth, never again withdraws entirely.

From the moment the circle is blessed with sincerity and precision, it ceases to be just a technical support and becomes a living field of listening, response, and transformation. The operator, then, no longer acts merely as an executor of formulas: they become a guardian of a territory where the spiritual presence manifests according to the invoked truth. To inhabit this consecrated space is, in itself, an exercise of inner vigilance and alignment with the most high. It is in this silence woven by elements, words, and intentions that the mystery begins to whisper—and the circle, once just a trace on the ground, becomes a place where the invisible reveals itself.

Chapter 6
Blessing of the Perfumes

In the context of the *Heptameron*, perfumes are not mere decorative fragrances or sensory additives; they are liturgical instruments of the highest symbolic and functional value. Their function transcends the physical: they translate the invisible into tangible presence. When the operator places grains of resin or dried leaves on the incandescent charcoal, they are not just initiating a process of combustion, but activating a channel of communication between distinct planes of being. The smoke that is released carries, encoded in its wisps, intentions, silent words, hidden desires, vows, and prayers.

At the heart of the *Heptameron's* ritualistics, this smoke becomes an intermediary agent—a fleeting yet powerful entity that travels the in-between worlds with a defined mission: to announce to the higher plane that a call has been made. Just as the candle is not merely light but presence, and the salt is not merely a mineral but a boundary and protection, the perfume is transition: from the dense to the subtle, from the body to the spirit, from the human to the angelic.

There is, in this process, a ritual aesthetic and ethic. The choice of ingredients is not made out of personal preference, but out of vibrational consonance with the archangel of the day, with the ruling planet, with the spiritual quality one wishes to summon. When it is said that each day of the week has its specific perfumes, it speaks of a celestial aromatic language, where each essence corresponds to a note in an invisible hymn. Frankincense, for example, when burned on a Sunday, opens the solar portals and strengthens the axis of the will. Myrrh, used on Mondays, immerses the operator in lunar waters, making them receptive to the subtle messages of the unconscious and to visions.

The preparation of these perfumes, therefore, is an act of devotional alchemy. Grinding the resin with a pestle, crushing dried petals, measuring the elements with attention and respect—all of this constitutes a ritual preamble that already begins to elevate the mind and heart. The perfume starts to act even before it is burned, for in preparing it, the magician already attunes themself to the spiritual intelligence it will represent.

During ritual use, the perfume serves as an offering in itself, but also as a vibrational mirror: it reflects the operator's intention and amplifies it. When burned at the beginning of the rite, it purifies the space, breaking down harmful influences. When offered at the moment of invocation, its smoke becomes a throne for the called presences, a subtle vehicle upon which the entities of light can rest. And when inhaled with reverence, it modifies the operator themself, tuning their perception, sharpening their intuition, opening their inner channels for contact with the invisible.

This contact does not occur only in mystical terms. The perfume affects the subtle biology of the being. It acts on the nervous system, regulates breathing, and influences the heart rate. It is no wonder that so many ancient traditions considered aromas to be bearers of soul—the Hebrew *ruach*, the Greek *pneuma*, the Indian *prāṇa*—all words that also mean breath, spirit, vital essence.

In the rite of the *Heptameron*, this breath takes on an aromatic form. And like all breath, it needs intention to gain direction. The simple burning of a resin, without purpose, is just smoke. But when the operator offers it with concentration and devotion, it transforms into a message. The censer, then, ceases to be a physical instrument and becomes a portable altar, a sacred furnace, a crucible where the invisible condenses and the visible dissolves.

This is the mystery of the blessing of the perfumes: to make the air a sacrament. To make the invisible a messenger. To convert the ephemeral fragrance into an enduring presence. It is not just about burning substances, but about consecrating the space between worlds—that brief and eternal instant when the aroma touches the soul and the soul, in silence, responds.

- The Spiritual Meaning of Perfumes

The presence of perfume in spiritual rites is not a mere sensory artifice, but an ancestral testament to a sacred language that precedes words. From the dawn of humanity's religious history, aromas have been perceived as invisible offerings, as prayers that need no voice to ascend to the heavens. When an Egyptian priest burned frankincense in the temples of Heliopolis, when the Hebrew high priest passed through the veil of the Holy of Holies carrying a censer, or when, in Hindu temples, jasmine petals and sandalwood sticks were offered before a divine image—in all these cases, there was a common intuition: aroma is spirit in subtle form.

This perception is profoundly consistent with the foundations of the *Heptameron*, whose liturgy seeks to restore an alliance between the worlds, using natural elements as bridges between the visible and the invisible. In this context, perfume becomes one of the most potent instruments. It acts simultaneously on the physical, emotional, and spiritual planes, and its action is almost instantaneous. The smoke does not need to be translated; it is understood directly by the celestial intelligences, as it carries in its vibration the intention of the heart that offered it.

In the tradition of the *Heptameron*, each day of the week is not just a unit of time, but a vibrational field governed by a specific celestial force. These fields have their colors, their symbols, their metals, and—especially relevant here—their aromas. Thus, the choice of perfumes for each day is not decorative, but essential. It anchors the ritual within the corresponding astrological and angelic current, harmonizing the operator with the spiritual quality of that frequency. To burn myrrh on a Monday, for example, is like speaking the language of the Moon and the archangel Gabriel, while burning cinnamon and nutmeg on a Thursday is to open the paths of Jupiter and Sachiel.

This system of correspondence is not arbitrary. It was revealed and confirmed by generations of magicians and mystics who observed, with rigor and devotion, the real effects of fumigation within rituals. Some aromas expand consciousness and favor visions; others ground and strengthen the energy field. There are those that cleanse and dissipate harmful presences, and those that attract luminous entities. It all depends on the combination of the perfume, the moment, and the intention.

In the Bible, God not only accepts incense: He commands its creation with precise formulas, instructing Moses to gather storax, onycha, galbanum, and pure frankincense in equal parts—a perfume reserved exclusively for sacred worship. This care with proportion and purity is not a mere divine whim, but a profound teaching: the aroma offered to the Most High must be worthy of what one seeks to receive. The same principle appears in the Book of Revelation, where angels offer incense before the throne as a symbol of the prayers of the righteous. The aroma, here, is both mediation and testimony.

In the practice of the *Heptameron*, the lit censer with the consecrated perfumes is what makes the ritual environment a true temple. Even before any word is pronounced, the smoke has already begun to act, delimiting the space, purifying the air, and attracting the celestial presences. It is common for the operator to feel, at this moment, a subtle change in the environment: the air becomes denser, as if populated by something invisible; thoughts quiet down; breathing deepens. This is the first sign that the bridge has been established.

Therefore, to understand the spiritual meaning of perfumes is to understand that they are not adornments, but messengers. They are winds laden with soul, carrying with them the essence of what the operator wishes to communicate to the spiritual world. To use them with reverence is to acknowledge their power. To prepare them with devotion is to participate in the great tradition of the alchemists of the spirit. To burn them with pure intention is, ultimately, to transform the air into prayer.

- Perfumes by Day of the Week

Below is the traditional correspondence between the days, archangels, and perfumes:

- Sunday (Sun – Michael): Frankincense, benzoin, golden resin. This is the day of full light, spiritual authority, and protective angelic presence. Frankincense, with its noble and penetrating aroma, symbolizes the ascent of consciousness and the nobility of the spirit. Benzoin, sweet and resinous, elevates and gladdens the environment, opening the heart to trust. Golden resin—such as gum arabic infused with gold powder or translucent yellow resins—exalts the solar brilliance, attracting forces of success, courage, and discernment. The mixture of these perfumes creates a field of luminous vitality and affirmation of the higher will.
- Monday (Moon – Gabriel): Myrrh, white amber, camphor. Under the domain of the Moon, this day

invites introspection, inner listening, and emotional purification. Myrrh, bitter and dense, allows one to dive into the deep waters of the soul, dissolving grievances and favoring revelatory dreams. White amber, soft and ethereal, stabilizes the aura and protects against confused or scattered energies. Camphor, with its cold and purifying nature, dissipates negative influences and prepares the operator's sensitive field for receiving angelic messages. It is the ideal combination for oracular practices, psychic cleansing, and dream work.

- Tuesday (Mars – Samael): Sulfur, dracaena resin, dried rue. This is the day of internal and external battles, of invoked courage, and of imposed justice. Sulfur, an alchemical symbol of the igneous and purifying principle, breaks through blockages and repels astral larvae. Dracaena resin, or "dragon's blood," fortifies energetic boundaries and acts as an intense vibrational defense. Dried rue, traditionally used in blessings and exorcisms, reinforces protection against envy, witchcraft, and all forms of spiritual attack. Together, these elements form a field of strong and direct action, ideal for deep cleansings and operations of severance.

- Wednesday (Mercury – Raphael): Sandalwood, lavender, bay leaves. The day of Mercury is governed by the word, by healing, and by the connection between worlds. Sandalwood, with its warm and meditative aroma, promotes spiritual elevation and mental stability. Lavender, light and floral, harmonizes the mental field, calming scattered thoughts and favoring inner listening. Bay leaves, consecrated to Apollo and oracles, expand subtle perception and favor visions and intuitions. This combination is indicated for rituals of communication with spirits, consecrations of instruments, and energetic healing work.

- Thursday (Jupiter – Sachiel): Cinnamon stick, orange peel, nutmeg. Jupiter rules expansion, abundance, and benevolent wisdom. Cinnamon stick, warm and stimulating, attracts prosperity and enthusiasm. Orange peel, citrusy and solar, promotes joy, the opening of paths, and fluidity in relationships. Nutmeg, spicy and aromatic, acts as a spiritual catalyst, accelerating processes of achievement. This combination forms a field of positive magnetism, ideal for petitions for material blessings, expansion of personal influence, and connection with spiritual masters.
- Friday (Venus – Anael): Rose petals, dried jasmine, vegetable musk. The day of Venus is consecrated to love, beauty, and harmony in relationships. Rose petals, especially red and white rose, evoke pure love, devotion, and the delicacy of the soul. Dried jasmine, with its enveloping scent, awakens the higher senses and favors gentle meditative states. Vegetable musk, rare and profoundly sensual, anchors sacred pleasure and intensifies the operator's presence in

their own body. This perfume celebrates the union between desire and spirit, being ideal for rituals of reconciliation, enchantment, and self-acceptance.
- Saturday (Saturn – Cassiel): Cypress, black amber, aromatic vegetable charcoal. Saturn rules boundaries, time, structure, and inner silence. Cypress, with its dry and deep aroma, invites meditation on finitude and moral firmness. Black amber, thick and mysterious, favors contact with ancestors and the guardians of portals. Aromatic vegetable charcoal serves as a base to support the other essences, but also acts as an element of transmutation, absorbing dense energies. This trio composes an atmosphere of recollection, discernment, and purification of inner shadows.

These mixtures should be made with natural substances—resins, dried leaves, flowers, and oils—and never with artificial or synthetic products. The vibration of the natural is essential for spiritual communication.
- The Choice and Preparation of the Ingredients

When preparing the perfumes, the operator must do so with reverence. The simple act of grinding herbs, mixing resins, or cutting petals is already a prayer in motion. Every gesture, every touch on the aromatic matter, must be permeated with intention and presence. The operator is not just a mixer of ingredients, but an officiant before the altar of nature. The preparation begins with inner silence, a gathering of attention so that the external act reflects an internal disposition appropriate to the sacred.

- Choose the ingredients in advance and, if possible, gather them directly from nature. By harvesting with one's own hands, the operator participates in the plant's life cycle, recognizing its origin and giving thanks for its donation. This gesture establishes an alliance with the vegetable and elemental kingdoms. It is important to gather only what is necessary, preferably at auspicious times and under favorable celestial conditions, respecting the lunar cycles and the astrological correspondence of the day.
- Keep the perfumes in amber glass or dark ceramic containers. The choice of container is not trivial: amber glass protects against light and stabilizes the vibrational composition of the ingredients, while dark ceramic maintains temperature and insulates against external interference. These containers should be reserved exclusively for ritualistic use and never employed for profane purposes.
- Store in a dry place, away from strong odors and direct sunlight. Perfumes easily absorb vibrational impressions. Environments contaminated by synthetic smells, intense noises, or chaotic energies can affect their purity. The storage place should be quiet, clean, and, if possible, consecrated, functioning as a resting chamber where the aromas mature spiritually.
- Do not mix perfumes from different days. Each mixture is an entity in itself, with its own purpose, rulership, and energy. Mixing ingredients from

different days causes vibrational dissonance, weakening the ritual effect. The magician should avoid improvisations and respect the celestial scheme of the *Heptameron*, treating each composition as a spiritual being with a specific identity and function.

- Before each use, mentally review its function and consecration. The simple gesture of recalling the consecration renews the energetic link with the perfume. The operator should bring to mind the original intention of the preparation, reactivating the spiritual memory of the mixture. This subtle act revives the compound's strength and aligns it with the work to be performed, reinforcing its effectiveness.
- The Consecration of the Perfumes

Just as the circle needs to be blessed before use, so too must the perfumes undergo a rite of consecration. The objective is to make them fit to serve as intermediaries between the worlds. This consecration is not just a ceremonial protocol, but a profound process of elevating matter. Through it, the ingredients—though natural and already vibrant—are sealed with a clear spiritual purpose, recognized and activated on the invisible plane as instruments of light.

The consecration links the perfume to the operator, to the day, and to the ruling angel. It confers a vibrational identity and a spiritual signature. After this rite, the mixture can no longer be treated as something common: it becomes the bearer of a call, a silent presence that, when burned, activates the space between worlds. The consecration is the baptism of the fragrance—the moment when it ceases to be just an aroma and becomes a living offering.

- Necessary materials:
    - The container with the perfumes prepared for the day of the ritual;
    - Lustral water (holy water with consecrated salt);
    - A lit censer with live charcoal;
    - A lit white candle;
    - The grimoire with the prayer of consecration.

Each of these elements must be ready and arranged in advance, as, in the rite of the *Heptameron*, the order and clarity of gestures are fundamental. The container with the perfumes represents the heart of the operation: it holds the ingredients that, once activated, will serve as a link between the worlds. The lustral water is the agent of initial purification, capable of removing any impure vibrational impressions or residual energetic remnants from the materials. It should be prepared according to traditional instructions, mixing clean water with consecrated salt and pronouncing the appropriate words of blessing.

The censer with live charcoal symbolizes the transmuting fire—the same that on the ancient altar consumed the sacrifices and made the smoke rise as a witness to the offering. The charcoal should be lit with attention and in silence, as if awakening a sleeping guardian. The white candle, simple and pure, marks the presence of the divine light in the rite and should remain lit throughout the consecration, illuminating the space and witnessing the intention.

Finally, the grimoire with the prayer of consecration is not just a manual, but a living presence of the tradition. It contains the words already consecrated by centuries of ritual use, and its reading must be done with solemnity, as if invoking an ancient spiritual current. Together, these elements form the minimal altar, the sacred space where the perfume will cease to be merely an aromatic substance and become a messenger of the spirit.

- Step-by-step of the consecration:
    1. Ritual posture: Put on your tunic, enter a state of silence and concentration. Place the perfumes before the altar or the censer. Before any action, it is essential for the operator to come into harmony with themself and the surrounding space. The tunic, more than a garment, is a sign of detachment from profane identities and alignment with the sacred office. The silence should not only be external but, above all, internal: it is the emptiness that prepares the ground for the mystery. The arrangement of the perfumes on the altar must be done with care and respect, as if presenting an offering that will be elevated to the sacred.
    2. Aspersion: With the sprig of hyssop or rosemary, sprinkle the perfume three times with the lustral water, saying: "May this

substance be purified of all unwanted influence, visible or invisible, by the virtue of the Name that is above every name." Aspersion is a universal gesture of consecration. The number three evokes the divine triad, and the sprig—a symbol of connection with the vegetable kingdom—serves as a bridge between the consecrated liquid and the container. The use of hyssop directly recalls biblical purification practices, while rosemary, besides being sacred in various traditions, enhances spiritual clarity. The pronounced formula should be intoned with firmness and reverence, as if sealing the substances with an invisible shield.

3. Elevation and invocation: Hold the container with both hands and raise it to the level of your heart or forehead, reciting: "Eternal and Almighty God, Creator of aromas and Lord of essences, deign to bless these perfumes, that they may become instruments of light, of purification, and of elevation. May no impure presence be able to resist their fragrance. May their smoke be a shield and their essence, a path. May the angels we invoke recognize in them the call of the soul. So be it." This is the apex of the rite. Raising the container to the heart establishes an emotional communion; to the forehead, a mental and spiritual

communion. The prayer should be read or recited in a solemn tone, with full awareness that one is making a direct link between heaven and earth. Each phrase of the invocation acts as a vibrational key, summoning higher forces to inhabit and transform the offered substance.

4. Reciprocal fumigation: After the prayer, place a small portion of the perfume on the charcoal. When the smoke rises, pass the rest of the ingredients through the smoke three times, in the form of a cross. The fumigation seals the prayer with action. By offering the first portion to the charcoal, the operator initiates the cycle of sacralization by fire. The resulting smoke is no longer common: it is a bearer of blessing. By passing the container through the smoke in the form of a cross, an invisible seal of light is inscribed upon the mixture, marking it as a consecrated instrument. The number three, again, reinforces the triple dimension of the rite: body, soul, and spirit; intention, word, and action.

5. Final seal: Make the sign of the cross over the container and say: "This perfume is consecrated to the service of the angels of light, by the will of the Most High." This final gesture affirms the pact made during the rite. The sign of the cross belongs not only to one tradition but represents the

intersection between the planes, the meeting of the vertical and the horizontal, of the divine and the human. The final proclamation should be made with firmness and inner peace, for at this moment the substance is transformed into a messenger of light. From then on, it no longer belongs to the ordinary world: it has become a sacrament of the air, ready to serve in the rites of the spirit.

After this, the perfumes are ready to be used in the corresponding ritual.

- The Use of Perfumes During the Ritual
The perfumes should be burned:
- At the beginning of the rite, for the purification of the environment;
- During the main prayers, as an aromatic offering;
- At the moment of conjuration, as a vehicle for vibrational elevation.

These three moments outline the liturgical arc of aromatic use within the rite of the *Heptameron*. At the beginning, the smoke acts as an invisible broom, sweeping away accumulated emotional and spiritual residues from the environment, breaking up stagnant thought-forms, and neutralizing dissonant presences. At this point, the operator should remain attentive to the expanding aroma, allowing it to act not only on the space but also on their own inner disposition.

During the main prayers, the perfume ceases to be an instrument of cleansing and becomes an offering: it is as if the operator's heart rises with the smoke, carrying in its spirals the silent vows, the invoked names, and the plea for divine hearing. The censer should be lifted slowly, circling the altar or the magic circle with rhythmic movements, as if drawing the contours of an invisible temple in the air. The smoke here is both incense and censer: it is an altar in motion.

At the moment of conjuration, when the operator pronounces the sacred names, traces seals, or performs formal invocations, the function of the perfume intensifies. It acts as a vibrational vehicle: its fragrance permeates the interstices of reality, opening subtle channels that facilitate the descent of the summoned angelic or spiritual presences. At this stage, the operator should be in the center of the smoke, breathing consciously, with reverence, allowing each inhalation to align them more deeply with the spiritual frequency of the work.

The smoke creates a symbolic "column" between the circle and the heavens. The operator should place themselves within it, inhaling with reverence and allowing the aroma to envelop their auric field. This column—invisible to ordinary eyes, but perceptible to the sensitive—is like an axis mundi: it connects the point of the ritual with the dwelling place of the spirit. It is both bridge and channel, aerial root and thread of return.

The intensity of the fumigation should be sufficient to create presence, but never suffocating. The air must remain breathable and subtle. Excessive smoke distracts attention, obscures perception, and can cause physical discomfort. The ideal is for the perfume to dance in the air like a light, subtly dense veil, capable of holding within it the memory of the operator's intention.

- Aromas and States of Consciousness

Each aroma possesses a vibrational signature that acts upon the subtle body and psyche of the operator:

- Frankincense: spiritual elevation, clarity of intention.
- Myrrh: introspection, emotional purification.
- Lavender: mental balance, protection against distractions.
- Cinnamon: enthusiasm, opening of the heart.
- Rose: unconditional love, gentleness of presence.
- Cypress: detachment, inner firmness.

These correspondences are not merely symbolic, but experiential. The repetition of rites with the same aromas creates, over time, a spiritual memory that is inscribed in the magician's energy field. Constant practice reveals that certain perfumes induce specific meditative states, others activate sensitive regions of the subtle body, and some evoke deep feelings of reconnection, peace, or strength.

Knowing how to interpret these effects helps the magician to choose and apply the appropriate perfume for each operation and state of soul. Sometimes, what is sought is not just spiritual activation, but grounding, the healing of an emotion, or the untying of an energetic knot. The correct perfume then becomes an invisible ally, a silent master, that leads the operator to regions of being where words cannot reach, but where the aroma speaks—and transforms.

Therefore, the conscious use of perfumes should be part of the magician's training. Noting reactions, observing dreams, and perceiving how each perfume acts on one's personal field are practices complementary to the rite. An olfactory diary can become a silent and precious grimoire, where unique patterns are revealed: perhaps lavender always brings prophetic dreams; perhaps jasmine opens the channels of inner listening with greater ease; perhaps sandalwood silences fears even before the invocation. These records build a subtle cartography of the magician's soul in relation to aromas.

Furthermore, there are perfumes that function as true mental anchors. When used regularly in specific spiritual contexts, they begin to instantly evoke the desired state of consciousness. Just as a physical temple can be recognized by its sacred architecture, the magician's inner temple can be accessed more quickly when a familiar aroma ignites the same neural connections linked to recollection, invocation, or contemplation.

This anchoring mechanism also serves as a shield: by using a consecrated perfume in critical moments or in hostile environments, the operator automatically reactivates the vibrational structure of the practice, protecting themselves from external influences and maintaining their psychic integrity. The simple act of inhaling the aroma becomes an act of spiritual remembrance—and, therefore, of power.

This psychological dimension of fumigation should not be underestimated. It reveals that the rite is not limited to the symbolic or energetic plane but penetrates the body and mind with concrete and measurable effects. A well-trained magician knows how to use this bridge wisely, recognizing in perfumes not only spiritual allies but also catalysts for their own inner transformation.

Perfume is the invisible breath of ceremonial magic. It not only purifies and scents: it communicates, elevates, and consecrates. In the *Heptameron*, its importance is central, as it prepares the atmosphere, attracts the angels, and wards off all that is not light. The blessing of the perfumes is, therefore, a rite of sacralization of the air—the most subtle and least visible element, but also the most pervasive.

By raising the smoke with pure intention, the operator performs an ancient gesture: that of transforming matter into an offering, aroma into prayer, presence into invocation. The censer thus becomes a portable altar, and the charcoal, a spark of the eternal fire. And the air—often forgotten, invisible, common—is revealed, in the alchemy of fumigation, as the privileged path to the invisible, the silent road along which the angels walk to the circle.

To treat perfumes as one treats the sacred word is to recognize that, in the silence of their ascent, there is a speech that needs no language. The smoke that rises from the censer carries not only the formulas and vows, but also the soul of the rite, the warmth of the intention, the memory of the devotional gesture. When a consecrated aroma spreads through the air, it seals the space with an invisible pact and invites the spirit to listen. Thus, each fumigation becomes more than a preparatory act: it becomes the very beginning of manifestation, the instant when the invisible already begins to respond, with fragrance as a bridge and the air as an altar.

Chapter 7
Exorcism of the Fire

Although invisible to the eyes, the fire that is kindled in the censer carries within it multiple layers of signification. In its pulsating glow dwell not only atoms in combustion but also the ancestral archetypes that have shaped humanity's relationship with the divine. Every spark that leaps from the lit charcoal echoes a primordial pact between the creature and the Creator—a pact that must be reiterated, purified, and re-consecrated with each rite. Negligence in this initial gesture, however subtle it may seem, compromises the vibrational integrity of the entire operation that will follow. Fire, when treated as a mere functional resource, loses its priestly vocation and becomes blind, erratic, and vulnerable to the wandering forces of the invisible plane.

Therefore, the exorcism of the fire is not a ceremonial addition but a structural necessity. The ritual purification of the flame must precede any spiritual use, just as one washes the altar before placing offerings upon it. The origin of the fire matters. Its spiritual genealogy, so to speak, must be redirected to the Most High. The operator needs to become aware that the fire they handle is not the same as the one that boils water or lights an oven. It is another fire: a fire that has been called, set apart, and vested with meaning. In many wisdom traditions, this type of fire is known as "living fire"—not because it is literally animate, but because it acts in consonance with the invisible order.

The practice of exorcism, in this context, functions as a kind of baptism of fire. Not in an allegorical sense, but as a rite of passage: that which was profane becomes sacred. That which was indiscriminate gains purpose. The moment the flame is sprinkled, invoked, and dedicated, it begins to respond to another logic—it no longer burns out of inertia, but out of consecrated intention. This transfiguration is both a vibrational change and a symbolic repositioning. And, like any living symbol, this consecrated fire acts in layers: it heats the incense, yes, but it also orders the psyche, magnetizes the environment, and sustains the threshold between worlds.

There is also a less visible and equally decisive aspect: the memory of the fire. Despite being an ephemeral element, fire retains impressions. The lit ember carries energetic records—both from the matter of its origin and from the context in which it is handled. Therefore, the purity of the charcoal, the dignity of the candle that lights it, the operator's state of mind, and even the words spoken during the rite have a real impact on the quality of the fire that will arise. To treat this process with negligence or haste compromises its effectiveness. An impure fire can produce a heavy, scattered smoke that does not elevate but obscures. A consecrated fire, however, becomes a conductor, a bridge, a herald of the invisible.

In many esoteric lineages, there is even a recommendation to listen to the fire. This does not mean hearing literal sounds, but perceiving its symbolic "speech": the speed at which it burns, the color of its flame, the crackles it emits, the shape it assumes. All of this can be interpreted as a response. A fire that is slow to catch may indicate internal resistance. A charcoal that extinguishes quickly may suggest energetic interruptions. A sudden flare-up may signal a spiritual presence. Thus, fire is not just a resource in the rite—it is also an oracle. A burning mirror where the invisible reflects its language.

More than that: the exorcism of the fire inscribes the magician into a tradition. By repeating the ancestral words, by performing the gestures with reverence, the operator aligns themselves with a current of power that surpasses their individuality. They are no longer alone. The flame they consecrate is, at the same time, a witness and a channel. A witness to their deepest intention. A channel for the presence they wish to invoke. In this sense, the fire becomes a conscious intermediary: it translates the verticality of prayer into heat, the aspiration of the soul into perfume, the clarity of purpose into light. And like any true intermediary, it cannot be profaned.

It is this reoriented flame that will sustain the rite of the *Heptameron*. Without it, everything becomes mechanical. With it, each ritual step gains weight, resonance, and vitality. The consecration of the fire, therefore, is more than a protocol: it is the threshold that separates a magical gesture from mere technical manipulation. It is the dawn of the rite. The first lit altar. The sign that something greater has already begun to descend.

- Fire as Symbol and Power

Fire is one of the most powerful archetypes in human experience. It illuminates, warms, transforms, but also destroys and devours. It is the most unstable and untamable element, frequently associated with the spirit, the will, and the divine presence. In ancient traditions, fire was considered a gift from the gods, and lighting it was a solemn act.

The ambiguous nature of fire, capable of both creating and destroying, makes it a symbol par excellence of deep spiritual processes. It represents passage, the threshold, the crossing between states. The burning fire is not just matter in combustion but an image of a mystery: the continuous transformation of substance and soul. It is no coincidence that initiatory trials in so many ancient orders involve the mastery or symbolic crossing of fire—whether as a literal flame or as a metaphor for the transfiguring will.

In the ritual context, fire operates as a mediator. It consumes the raw matter—the incense, the herb, the residue—and translates it into smoke, aroma, and invocation. The verticality of its natural ascent makes it a messenger par excellence: it carries the invisible with it, dissolves forms, and opens the space. Thus, it is natural that it be associated with the spirit and higher consciousness. Where there is consecrated fire, there is presence. Where the flame dances, the atmosphere changes. The light it projects is not only physical: it is psychic and animic, capable of revealing or protecting, of activating or transmuting.

In the Bible, fire is a sign of God's presence—as in the burning bush of Moses (Exodus 3), which burned without being consumed, an expression of ineffable transcendence; on the altar of Elijah (1 Kings 18), where fire from heaven consumes the sacrifice as divine confirmation; or at Pentecost (Acts 2), where tongues of fire rest upon the apostles, marking the beginning of a mission illuminated by the Holy Spirit. In all these episodes, the fire is not destructive, but affirmative: it authenticates, consecrates, and legitimizes.

However, the same fire that illuminates also tests. It is a fire of judgment, like that which purifies metals. The prophets speak of a God who refines with fire, not to punish, but to prepare. This purifying aspect is essential in spiritual practice: that which passes through fire becomes more essential, more pure, more true. In the *Heptameron*, the fire that will burn under the perfumes needs to be under spiritual dominion, for it is through it that prayers are elevated and environments are impregnated with sanctity. It is not enough to burn: one must burn with meaning, with direction, with reverence.

Therefore, lighting the ritual fire is not a trivial act. It is like opening a gate between worlds. Fire without exorcism is a door open to any presence; consecrated fire is a sealed door, where only that which has been called with righteousness may enter. To master fire does not mean to control it as one masters a tool, but to recognize it as a living presence that demands respect, listening, and care. And so, the magician, by lighting the flame with sacred words, not only activates an element: they inscribe themselves in a chain of meaning that comes from the gods, the prophets, the initiates. The ember becomes an altar, and the heat, an invocation.

- Why Exorcise the Fire?

Common fire is neutral. It can be used for good or for ill, and its heat can either prepare a remedy or fuel destruction. By exorcising the fire, the operator ensures that the flame used in the ceremony does not carry remnants of others' intentions, impure energies, or unwanted vibrational memories.

But there is an even deeper reason for this practice: fire, due to its subtle and penetrating nature, is highly receptive to the psychic and spiritual influences of the environment. It absorbs impressions, reverberates intentions, and amplifies desires. A fire lit without consciousness, even if visually identical to a consecrated one, can become a vehicle for disordered forces, scattering or even corrupting the vibrational quality of the rite. To exorcise the fire is, thus, to protect it—and oneself—from invisible contaminations.

Furthermore, the act of exorcising the fire constitutes a form of reorientation. It breaks with the automatism of mechanical action and inserts the gesture of lighting into a sacred context, awakening in the operator a state of presence and reverence. The fire is no longer a passive tool: it becomes an active collaborator in the rite, a conscious partner in the magical operation.

At the same time, to consecrate the fire is to surrender this element to the divine hierarchy, so that it does not act by its own blind force but as an extension of the sacred will. It is to transform the fire into a spiritual minister, and not a simple physical phenomenon.

This consecration inscribes it in a broader chain of meanings, causing its combustion to translate, on the physical plane, the invisible light that guides and sustains the ritual work. The fire begins to burn as a sign of alliance. Its heat becomes a spiritual touch. Its light, a silent word from the Most High. Thus, by exorcising and consecrating the flame, the operator not only purifies the matter—they also reconfigure their own position before the mystery they invoke.

- Fire in the Rite of the Heptameron

The consecrated fire assumes a fundamental role in the structure of the *Heptameron*, carrying within it multiple functions that go beyond the mere practical aspect of burning incenses. Its presence is multifaceted and indispensable for the effectiveness and depth of the rite.

- It heats the censer, making it possible to burn the perfumes, whose smoke invokes and purifies. This function, though apparent, is the material basis for the use of fire in the ritual. Without the appropriate and constant temperature provided by the charcoal ember, the combustion of the incense would not occur as expected. The rising smoke is, therefore, the sensible vehicle of invocation—an element that not only transports prayers but also

cleanses the space, warding off dense or dissonant energies.
- It symbolizes the presence of the spirit, illuminating the space and representing the light of consciousness. The flame is not simply an instrument but a living symbol of the manifestation of the spirit in the rite. It brings light where there is shadow, clarifies the consciousness of the operator and those present, and establishes an atmosphere conducive to communication with the divine. Its silent dance mirrors the fluidity of the soul and the dynamics of the spiritual will in action.
- It marks the intensity of the magical operation, functioning as a symbolic thermometer of spiritual presence and activity. More than a mere physical element, the fire reveals the state of the rite. A vibrant and stable flame indicates harmony between the planes and the success of the invocation; a flickering or unstable flame may signal imbalances, resistance, or interference. Thus, the fire becomes a living indicator, allowing the operator to adjust their posture, intentions, and actions as necessary for the full realization of the work.

Therefore, this is not a technical detail: fire is the central axis that sustains the entire ritualistics of the *Heptameron*. Its care requires reverence, attention, and adequate preparation so that its manifestation may be full and effective.

- Preparation of the Fire: Material Requirements

Before beginning the exorcism, the operator must gather and prepare the elements with rigor and respect:
- A vessel or censer, preferably of new clay, as indicated by the grimoire, to avoid physical and energetic contamination. Metal containers with handles may be used, provided they are exclusive to ritual use and properly consecrated.
- Natural vegetable charcoal, without chemical additives, that burns slowly and steadily, ensuring a clean and lasting flame.
- Metal tongs, indispensable for the safe handling of the charcoal, preventing accidents and maintaining the integrity of the ritual.
- An insulating stone or plate, to support the censer and prevent damage to the altar or ritual surface.
- A lit white candle, a symbol of the original light of the sacred fire, whose purity illuminates and protects the environment during preparation.
- Lustral water and a sprig of hyssop or rosemary, for the purifying aspersion that precedes and accompanies the rite.
- The Exorcism of the Fire: Complete Rite

The sequence of the rite is structured to establish the necessary spiritual connection, to purify and consecrate the fire, transforming it into a living channel of the divine will. This rite should be performed before the first use of the charcoal and, preferably, repeated at each new ceremony to maintain the quality and intensity of the ritual flame.

- 1. Silence and Centering

The operator positions themself before the censer with the unlit charcoal, wearing the ritual robe, seeking inner recollection and mental quietude. They light the white candle—which symbolizes the pure and primordial fire—and fix their gaze on it for a few seconds, absorbing its light and presence. With a centered mind, they direct their words in invocation:

"Lord of Light, You who are the fire that does not consume, the flame that purifies and illuminates, consecrate this light and this flame to Your service. May it not be an instrument of pride or vanity, but of truth and elevation."

- 2. Aspersion

The aspersion with the sprig of hyssop or rosemary is not a merely symbolic gesture but an act of purification that connects the fire to the higher spiritual hierarchy. The lustral water, charged with beneficial and consecrated energies, removes any trace of material or vibrational impurity, preparing the element to receive the sacred presence. By sprinkling the candle and the charcoal, the operator draws an invisible barrier against external influences, establishing a clean, protected, and sacred space. The words spoken at this moment are a direct invitation to the light, affirming the purpose of clarity and elevation for the fire, so that its flame may be not only physical but spiritual, and its smoke, a pure vehicle for the prayers that will rise.

- 3. Lighting of the Charcoal

The lighting of the charcoal represents the awakening of the consecrated fire, the transition from potential to active manifestation. Aided by the flame of the white candle, a symbol of primordial light and purity, the operator begins the process with care and reverence. Bringing the hands near without touching the forming ember is a gesture of respect and restraint, preserving the energy of the sacred moment. The prayer of exorcism pronounced is not just a command to ward off negative forces but a deep invocation of the divine fire as an eternal presence and guardian of truth. Each word is charged with intention, aligning the fire with the will of the Most High, protecting it from deviant influences, and ensuring that its flame is a reflection of the Supreme Light. The possibility of reciting psalms complements and strengthens the invocation, inserting the rite into the context of ancient spiritual tradition, where fire has always been a sign of the manifestation of the divine among humans.

- 4. Final Consecration

With the charcoal finally lit and the flame stable, the operator raises the censer, a gesture that symbolizes the complete surrender of the fire to sacred service. The words of consecration reinforce this surrender, explicitly declaring that the fire is dedicated to truth, service, and spiritual elevation. The smoke of the perfumes that will rise over this flame now carries not only aroma but the supplication and intention of the magician, elevating them to the invisible plane without a shadow of doubt or impurity. The placement of the censer in its definitive spot and the silence that follows are moments of contemplation and perception of the change in the energetic field, when the fire truly becomes a living channel of the divine will, ready to sustain and potentiate the entire ritual operation.

This ritual sequence is the foundation of the integrity and effectiveness of the entire rite of the *Heptameron*. Its attentive and conscious performance ensures that fire, an unstable and powerful element, is a faithful and luminous ally, and not a chaotic or dangerous force.

- Important Observations

Ritualistic practice demands rigorous care to preserve the purity and effectiveness of the consecrated fire. Never reuse extinguished charcoal from a previous ritual, as the energetic memory of the old fire may carry unwanted remnants that compromise the vibrational quality of the new rite. Each operation must begin with new fire, a symbol of renewal and the operator's present commitment to the spiritual hierarchy.

It is fundamental to avoid using liquid fuel lighters or any chemical products to light the charcoal. These agents contaminate the flame with foreign substances and dissonant energetic noise, weakening the clarity of the invocation. Always prefer wooden matches or the soft light of the consecrated white candle, means that maintain the purity and integrity of the ritual fire.

The censer must always be clean, free of accumulated residues that could burn and release impurities. The physical cleanliness reflects the energetic cleanliness of the space and the fire, ensuring that nothing interferes with the ascent of the smoke as a sacred vehicle. After the rite concludes, the ashes generated by the charcoal and incenses should be disposed of with respect and reverence—the ideal is to bury them in the earth or cast them into running water, allowing their natural return to the cycle of creation and preventing unwanted vibrational charges from remaining in the environment.

- Fire and the Operator's State of Mind

The dynamic and sensitive nature of fire causes it to respond directly to the magician's internal state. Disordered emotions, impatience, or distraction are reflected in the instability of the flame, making it difficult to light or to keep it alive and vibrant. Therefore, the act of lighting the ritual fire must be accompanied by a conscious posture that integrates body, mind, and spirit.

Breathing slowly and deeply helps to slow the internal rhythm, preparing the operator for the necessary elevation. The recitation of prayers, whether mental or verbal, establishes the appropriate vibrational field and strengthens the intention. Inner recollection, in turn, harmonizes the energy centers, aligning them with the higher will.

Fire does not hide imbalance; it reveals the real state of the operator and the environment. Therefore, observing the quality of the flame is also a form of self-knowledge and adjustment. The attentive magician perceives in the nuances of the fire subtle indicators that guide their path in the rite, allowing for corrections and deepenings that elevate the quality of the spiritual work.

- Fire as Guardian

The summoning of fire as a guardian is an ancestral practice that elevates the flame from a simple material element to a protective entity of the ritual space. By uttering words that appeal to the divine origin of fire—that flame which illuminated prophets and the righteous—the operator establishes a direct link with the celestial sphere, making the fire an active watchman against any unwanted interference. This invocation is not a mere formality: it endows the flame with a symbolic consciousness, transforming it into a sentinel that not only warms and consumes but also maintains energetic balance, warding off shadows and preserving the purity of the environment. By designating the fire as a guardian, the magician acknowledges it as an ally, a partner in the magical process, whose presence reinforces the integrity and security of the rite.

- Fire and the Angels

In the *Heptameron*, the smoke that rises from the consecrated fire serves as a vehicle for the evocation of angels, bringing the spiritual essence of these beings to the material plane. Many angels associated with fire are also symbolically represented by the element itself, reinforcing their intrinsic connection to the sacred flame. Michael, for example, an emblematic figure with his flaming sword, personifies the purifying power and spiritual protection attributed to fire. The presence of consecrated fire potentiates angelic manifestation, functioning as an amplifier of the celestial consciousness that manifests on the sensible plane. It is through the quality and purity of the flame that the operator can ensure the fidelity of this connection; an un-exorcised, impure, or neglected fire can attract conflicting presences, hindering the success of the rite.

Therefore, the exorcism of the fire is not limited to a ceremonial formality but is a vital act of energetic and spiritual alignment, an indispensable condition for a frank and safe dialogue with the angelic spheres.

- The Light in the Center of the Circle

Keeping a lit candle in the center of the ritual circle transcends the role of a simple luminous support; it acts as the axis that articulates and maintains the energetic cohesion of the sacred space. This flame, almost silent in its movement, is the visible expression of the operator's soul, the luminous reflection of their intention and concentration. Its glow is simultaneously a beacon and a mirror, projecting outward the magician's clarity and reflecting back their own inner state in a dynamic and continuous exchange.

The white color of the candle, far from being a random choice, symbolizes the primordial purity of spiritual light, the untarnished essence that permeates creation and sustains the divine order. Its formal simplicity, devoid of ornaments or excesses, allows this light to manifest with transparency, without interference, a direct bridge between the visible and the invisible. The holder, fixed and solid, is not a mere detail: it is the foundation that ensures the permanence of the flame, preventing it from flickering due to external or internal distractions, mirroring the stability sought in the operator.

By consecrating this candle with the same words and gestures as the exorcism of the fire, a vibrational quality is imprinted upon it that connects it to the higher spiritual hierarchy, making it a palpable extension of the sacred fire that dwells in the censer. Its constant presence throughout the rite acts as an energetic anchor, stabilizing the vibrations of the environment, repelling interference, and protecting the ritual field. The flame that burns there is not just a physical light but a living presence that sustains the threshold between worlds, keeping open the channel through which the summoned forces transit.

This central fire is a conscious surrender by the magician, a gesture that manifests the abandonment of randomness and mechanical control to welcome sacred order and purpose. By surrendering this flame to the light, the operator recognizes the fire as an interlocutor, an ally that can only fulfill its role if treated with respect, attention, and reverence. The ritual fire, therefore, ceases to be a mere unstable element and transforms into a pillar of spiritual stability, a partner that dialogues in silence and translates the verticality of prayer into light.

Within the magician's inner self, this internalized flame burns with the same intensity as the fire in the censer. The ember becomes an altar, a space of encounter and offering; the smoke, a prayer that rises laden with intentions; the heat, a living presence that confirms the connection with the divine. This deep integration between the external and internal fire symbolizes the passage from a simple rite to an experience of transfiguration, where the operator not only handles an element but allows themselves to be transformed by it.

To advance on this step of the ritual ladder is to recognize that fire demands not only technical mastery but a continuous learning of humility and service. It is an invitation for the magician to understand that the consecrated flame only remains alive as long as there is respect and surrender, for fire, in its essence, is a mirror of the soul itself: rebellious, luminous, powerful, and delicate. To learn to serve the fire is, ultimately, to learn to serve oneself, one's own light that burns silently in the center of the circle and within the heart.

The consecration of the fire is, in the final analysis, the consecration of the magical gesture itself. The ember that burns under the perfumes, the candle that illuminates the center of the circle, the flame that remains alive amidst the silence—all these manifestations reveal a single truth: without consecrated fire, there is no complete rite. He who lights it with reverence, who purifies it with a righteous intention, and who listens to it with inner attention, transforms the most volatile of elements into a stable foundation for the spiritual operation. Thus, fire ceases to be a risk or noise and becomes a voice, a presence, a sign that the sacred has already begun to respond.

Chapter 8
The Seven Days and Their Angels

The ritual structure of the *Heptameron* is organized according to a celestial logic that distributes spiritual forces throughout the seven days of the week. Each day is ruled by a planetary archangel, assisted by ministers and spirits of the air who, together, form an invisible hierarchy prepared to respond to the sincere call of the operator. This chapter presents this structure in depth, providing the practitioner with a clear spiritual cartography to guide their magical and liturgical operations.

The weekly arrangement in the *Heptameron* is more than a chronological division; it mirrors the organization of the cosmos according to an ancestral angelic order, where each day represents a distinct emanation of the divine will. The week becomes a mirror of the Tree of Life, where the classical planets occupy specific positions, transmitting attributes that are channeled by the celestial hosts. Thus, the ritualist not only chooses a convenient time but aligns with a cosmic energy flow that pulses in sync with the heavens. This attunement does not depend on blind faith, but on an inner listening that recognizes, with time and practice, the vibrational texture of each day.

The Sun, for example, in its solar majesty on Sunday, represents awakened consciousness, the light that reveals, warms, and protects. Its archangel, Michael, is not just a symbol of protection, but the mirror of spiritual righteousness in action, the sword that cuts through illusion and reorders the soul under truth. His domain involves both strength and nobility—it is he who prepares the operator for higher spiritual missions, reinforcing the integrity of the chosen path.

The Moon of Monday, ruled by Gabriel, delves into the subtle waters of the subconscious, of dreams, and of veiled messages. Here, the operator learns to listen in silence, to interpret signs, to recognize the value of emotions as messengers of something greater. Gabriel, the angel of annunciation, not only delivers celestial messages but also teaches the operator to become a pure channel for the truth that comes from within. His domain includes the memory of the soul, visions of the future, and the veils that cover intuition.

On Tuesday, Mars extends its fiery mantle under the command of Samael (or Camael, in some versions), whose force can be both destructive and liberating. He rules the fire of purification, of courage in the face of error, and of the strength that rises against inner oppression. Rituals under his influence require firmness, ethics, and detachment, for what is severed on this day does not return. Samael is the spiritual surgeon who removes what no longer serves, and his touch, though severe, is profoundly restorative.

Mercury, the planet of communication and knowledge, offers Wednesday as a day of learning and healing, under the tutelage of Raphael. This archangel unites knowledge with practice, intelligence with compassion. There is no true healing without understanding, nor wisdom without action. Raphael guides scholars, healers, and seekers who wish to unite theory and experience in an effective spiritual practice. His work manifests in small gestures as well as in great revelations.

Thursday, with Jupiter and Sachiel, is consecrated to divine generosity, spiritual growth, and higher justice. Here, the operator is called to recognize the fruits of the path, to share, to give thanks. Sachiel does not respond to greed, but to the abundance that flows from alignment with the common good. His rites are expansive, noble, and imbued with hope.

Venus, on Friday, offers the sweetness of Anael, the restorer of relationships and ambassador of universal love. His gifts include beauty, harmony, and reconciliation—not only between people but also between the various aspects of the psyche. To operate under Anael is to open oneself to the aesthetics of the soul, to the forgiveness that heals, to the tenderness that strengthens.

Finally, Saturday belongs to Saturn and the enigmatic Cassiel, the angel of time, of limits, and of silence. His lessons are profound, often challenging, as they demand discipline, patience, and self-knowledge. Cassiel teaches how to cut away excesses, to consolidate internal structures, and to respect the mystery that inhabits each phase of closure. He is the guardian of the passage, the counselor of those who know that to evolve, one must know how to let go.

By understanding this celestial architecture, the practitioner not only plans their rites more effectively but also educates their spiritual sensitivity to recognize when each force is most present. Time becomes a living ally, a luminous ladder towards the sacred.

- The Week as a Celestial Wheel

For the *Heptameron*, the week is not just a temporal unit—it is a spiritual mandala, a living sequence of angelic forces that circulate cyclically. Each day is imbued with a specific vibration, ruled by a higher intelligence, and aligned with the classical planets of Western astrology: the Sun, Moon, Mars, Mercury, Jupiter, Venus, and Saturn.

This weekly cycle unfolds like a cosmic liturgy, in which chronological time is converted into ritual time. Each day of the week becomes a vibrational doorway, a station of contact with specific divine attributes. The operator, by following this structure, not only aligns with a broader spiritual flow but also participates in a hidden harmony that permeates all spheres of being. The cyclical repetition of the days, far from being a mundane routine, transforms into an invisible hymn, where each note—each day—resonates with a distinct celestial quality.

This planetary distribution is not arbitrary but echoes the ancient models of Kabbalah, esoteric astrology, and Christian liturgy, in which each planet corresponds to a sphere of spiritual manifestation, a virtue, and a mission. The Tree of Life, with its sefirot, serves as a symbolic matrix for the organization of the days: the solar light of Tiferet manifests on Sunday; the intuitive flow of Yesod shines on Monday; the rigor of Geburah ignites Tuesday; the intelligence of Hod illuminates Wednesday; the benevolence of Chesed blesses Thursday; the gentleness of Netzach harmonizes Friday; and the structure of Binah solidifies Saturday.

The attentive operator learns, over time, to feel these nuances as if they were internal climates. It is not just about choosing a propitious day, but about preparing the body and mind as instruments receptive to the corresponding spiritual frequency. The ritual, thus, does not begin with the act of invocation, but with the sensitive listening that precedes the choice of time. The correct practice begins with silence and discernment: which force needs to be mobilized? Which virtue should be awakened? Time ceases to be linear and becomes a habitable space, a landscape to be traversed with reverence.

- How to Choose the Appropriate Day

Before presenting the angels and their spheres of action, it is important to understand that the operator should choose the day of their practice according to the intention of the operation. Each day opens a specific type of portal, adjusting the nature of the desired spiritual intervention. Here are some suggestions:

- Sunday: Illumination, protection, success, spiritual authority. A solar day, excellent for requesting clarity, blessings on endeavors, strengthening of the will, and consecrating tools related to spiritual leadership.

- Monday: Intuition, dreams, emotional reconciliation, motherhood. A lunar day, propitious for work with waters, memories, ancestors, and issues related to the soul and the sacred feminine.
- Tuesday: Courage, energy, purification, justice. Mars rules this day with impetus and challenge. Ideal for operations of liberation, ritual severing, and inner strengthening.
- Wednesday: Healing, learning, intelligence, communication. Under Mercury, this day favors all acts that require mental clarity, study, written elaboration, as well as blessings on therapeutic processes.
- Thursday: Prosperity, blessings, divine wisdom, leadership. Jupiter expands and stabilizes. Excellent for petitions for justice, material growth, and the consecration of long-range projects.
- Friday: Love, beauty, harmony, forgiveness. Ruled by Venus, it is a day consecrated to affections, aesthetics, and the healing of bonds. It favors pacts of love, celebrations, and practices of spiritual self-care.
- Saturday: Discipline, structure, exorcism, introspection. The weight of Saturn requires preparation and respect. Indicated for sealings, advanced protection, closure of cycles, and work with spiritual inheritances.

Each day has its own set of seals, prayers, perfumes, and invocations, described in the upcoming chapters. These elements should not be seen as mystical accessories but as vibrational keys that adjust the operator's field to the invoked spiritual presence. The correct choice of the day and instruments enhances the effectiveness of the rite and strengthens the attunement between intention and manifestation.

Here, we will concentrate on the archangels and their spheres of action. They are the conductors of the planetary forces, the greater ministers who translate the powers of the heavens into forms accessible to human consciousness. To know them is to be initiated into a celestial geography whose cartography now begins to be revealed.

SUNDAY — ARCHANGEL MICHAEL

- Planet: Sun
- Functions: Protection, courage, spiritual clarity, combatting evil
- Associated Colors: Gold, white, light yellow
- Perfumes: Frankincense, benzoin
- Ministers: Dardiel, Huratapal, Capriel

Michael is the warrior of light, defender of just causes, and purifier of inner and outer darkness. On Sunday, the circle is filled with his solar presence, firm and protective. It is an ideal day for:

- Consecrating new instruments
- Requesting help against obstacles
- Strengthening the soul for the spiritual path

The operator who invokes Michael places themselves under the aegis of divine justice, receiving not only protection but also an inner call to align with the truth that transcends personal interests.

Characteristics of the Sunday rite include:
1. An intense vibrational atmosphere—marked by clarity and the expansion of moral consciousness
2. A review of spiritual purposes—ideal for reconsecrating vows and reorganizing intention
3. Strengthening of the magical perimeter—Michael guards the limits of the circle, warding off unwanted presences
4. Active participation of the ministers—Dardiel, Huratapal, and Capriel operate with precision in rituals of purification and defense

Practical suggestions for this day:
- Wear light-colored or golden robes
- Use solar incenses like frankincense
- Carry solar symbols such as the lion, a golden disk, or a sword

Psalm 91, recited with reverence, intensifies spiritual protection, acting as a seal of light against adverse forces.

Michael is also:
- The great celestial exorcist—powerful in rituals of spiritual liberation
- The restorer of divine order—severs harmful bonds and dissolves deceptions
- The instructor of courage—inspires firmness to face fears and make spiritual decisions

It is recommended that rites initiated on this day give rise to a weekly spiritual cycle, in which Sunday functions as:
- The solar starting point
- The luminous root of the other operations

- Suggested Psalm: Psalm 91 — "He who dwells in the secret place of the Most High shall abide under the shadow of the Almighty..."

MONDAY — ARCHANGEL GABRIEL

- Planet: Moon
- Functions: Intuition, revelations, reconciliation, protection of the family
- Associated Colors: Silver, light blue, pearl
- Perfumes: Myrrh, white amber, camphor
- Ministers: Miel, Seraphiel, Madiel

Gabriel is the divine messenger, bearer of visions, prophetic dreams, and emotional comfort. Monday is propitious for:

- Work with memories and family reconciliation
- Practices for psychic opening and refined intuition
- Consecration of lustral water and rites of emotional purification

The lunar vibration that rules this day favors inner recollection, subtle listening, and perception of the unspoken. Gabriel, in his function as a sacred announcer, reveals what is hidden beneath the layers of the conscious mind. He acts as an interpreter of the signs that arrive in dreams, of the messages that are insinuated through silence, of the feelings that are not expressed in words.

The rite of Monday should be conducted with gentleness and surrender. By invoking Gabriel, the operator attunes to the archetypal waters of the soul, awakening the ability to listen with the heart and to recognize, in small gestures, the presence of the divine.

His action is fluid and enveloping, promoting an environment of acceptance and deep emotional healing.

Striking characteristics of the lunar operation:
- Oneiric expansion—ideal for working with dream diaries, dream incubation, and nocturnal revelations
- Restoration of bonds—excellent for family reconciliations, harmonizing maternal or feminine relationships
- Emotional purification—the use of lustral water consecrated under Gabriel intensifies the process of inner cleansing
- Intuitive development—practices of inner listening, meditative tarot, or symbolic clairvoyance are favored

Gabriel also presides over the processes of spiritual birth. He is the angel who announces beginnings—not only on the physical plane but also in the awakening of the soul. Therefore, Monday is a propitious time to sow intentions that require slow maturation, such as deep healings, new affective beginnings, and the gestation of creative projects.

For the ritual preparation of this day, it is recommended to:
- Wear robes in shades of silver, light blue, or pearl
- Burn gentle incenses like myrrh or white amber
- Keep the environment in semi-darkness or under low light, stimulating introspection

The presence of his ministers—Miel, Seraphiel, and Madiel—reinforces the aspects of sweetness, protection, and revelation. They act as softeners of intense emotions, creating space for the soul to reorganize in peace. The invocation of Gabriel also strengthens the domestic energy field, protecting the home, children, and affective ties.

- Suggested Psalm: Psalm 42 — "As the deer pants for the water brooks, so pants my soul for You, O God..."

TUESDAY — ARCHANGEL SAMAEL

- Planet: Mars
- Functions: Strength, purification, justice, confronting fear
- Associated Colors: Dark red, iron, black
- Perfumes: Sulfur, rue, dracaena
- Ministers: Baciel, Carviel, Zavael

Samael (or Camael, in milder versions) rules the forces of transformation by fire. His domain is that of direct action, necessary rupture, and confronting that which paralyzes. Tuesday is ideal for:

- Rites of liberation and spiritual purification
- Energetic defense and ceremonial exorcisms
- Breaking limiting patterns and strengthening the will

Samael's presence manifests with incandescent vigor, like a flaming blade that cuts the ties with what no longer serves. He is not destructive by impulse but surgical in his intervention. He acts with moral precision, demanding neutrality, discernment, and courage from the operator.

Main characteristics of works performed under his influence:

- Power of rupture and overcoming—Samael facilitates severing ties with addictions, chronic fears, and psychic prisons
- Increase of inner strength—awakens the fighting instinct and spiritual readiness in the face of visible and invisible attacks
- Impersonal justice—rites on this day favor ethical judgments and corrective actions in unbalanced situations
- Intense purification—ideal for cleansing spiritually contaminated environments or bodies afflicted by emotional miasmas

Samael requires the operator to be firm, centered, and detached from sentimental expectations. It is not a day for gentle or contemplative rituals, but for acts of decision and spiritual combat. The preparation must be rigorous: purification baths with strong herbs (like rue and rosemary), a light fast, and inner silence are recommended.

Practical suggestions for Tuesday:
- Wear dark-colored robes, with details in red or iron tones
- Utilize symbols like swords, spears, or runes of Mars (like Tiwaz)
- Burn strong incenses, like sulfur, and keep the space ventilated and well-delimited

The action of the ministers Baciel, Carviel, and Zavael amplifies the aspects of tactical action, aggressive protection, and dissolution of spiritual obstacles. They operate as guardians of the rite, ensuring that the invoked force manifests in a controlled and effective manner.

Samael is also a master of spiritual courage. His presence teaches that, often, true progress comes from the direct confrontation of pain, deceit, and doubt. He strengthens the operator's posture before internal adversaries, inviting them to overcome through the way of fire—both symbolic and real.

- Suggested Psalm: Psalm 18 — "I will love You, O LORD, my strength. The LORD is my rock and my fortress and my deliverer..."

WEDNESDAY — ARCHANGEL RAPHAEL

- Planet: Mercury
- Functions: Healing, learning, practical wisdom, writing
- Associated Colors: Green, light yellow, gray
- Perfumes: Sandalwood, lavender, bay leaf
- Ministers: Darquiel, Barachiel, Uriel (in some versions)

Raphael is the divine physician, the healer of bodies and souls. His presence on Wednesday illuminates the paths of knowledge, clear communication, and the integration of mind and spirit. This is the best day for:

- Consecrating medicines or natural remedies
- Requesting healing—physical, emotional, or spiritual
- Activating tools for writing, teaching, or mediation
- Seeking practical guidance for existential dilemmas

The energy of Mercury pulsates like a living bridge between worlds: between heaven and earth, between thought and action, between wisdom and expression. Raphael embodies this mediation with grace and efficacy. His work is silent but profound—he acts behind the scenes, organizing thoughts, untying mental knots, facilitating the assimilation of experiences, and fostering the blossoming of understanding.

Fundamental characteristics of works under his aegis:
- Clarity of expression—excellent for developing communicative skills, writing sacred texts, or composing inspired speeches
- Integration of knowledge—favors the fusion of spiritual study and daily life, revealing how to apply the sacred in the concrete
- Restoration of psychophysical balance—his blessings promote energetic recovery, relief from ailments, and harmony between body and mind
- Protection on journeys—whether physical or spiritual, any journey initiated under his protection tends to be safe and enriching

Raphael also rules the paths of deep learning, making Wednesday ideal for esoteric studies, symbolic readings, and meditative practices aimed at absorbing wisdom. He is the patron of those who teach with the heart and learn with humility.

Practical suggestions for this day:
- Wear robes in shades of green, light yellow, or gray

- Burn incenses like lavender, sandalwood, or bay leaves
- Keep consecrated writing tools nearby—diaries, grimoires, quills, special pencils
- Meditate with mercurial symbols or seals of Raphael, seeking connection with his field of healing and intelligence

His ministers—Darquiel, Barachiel, and Uriel—potentiate distinct aspects: Darquiel brings discernment, Barachiel brings subtle blessings, and Uriel, when present, kindles the flame of practical illumination. Together, they sustain a field that favors both curative introspection and the lucid application of acquired knowledge.

Raphael also helps to reveal the hidden causes of pain, whether physical or spiritual. He invites the operator to look honestly at their habits, thoughts, and emotions, offering tools for a gradual and compassionate inner reform.

- Suggested Psalm: Psalm 30 — "O LORD my God, I cried out to You, and You healed me..."

THURSDAY — ARCHANGEL SACHIEL
- Planet: Jupiter
- Functions: Prosperity, expansion, blessings, divine justice
- Associated Colors: Royal blue, purple, gold
- Perfumes: Cinnamon, nutmeg, orange peel
- Ministers: Asaliah, Nadiel, Velel

Sachiel is the angel of generous benevolence and of the higher order that manifests as justice and abundance. On Thursday, the temple is imbued with his

expansive presence, like a fertile field ready to receive the seeds of spiritual merit. This is the ideal day for:
- Petitions for financial stability and long-term projects
- Rituals of gratitude and conscious generosity
- Blessings upon just contracts, alliances, and oaths
- Consecration of symbols of power and spiritual authority

The influence of Jupiter is expressed with solemnity and expansion. It is the vibration of confidence, of faith in the invisible order that rewards what is in harmony with the greater good. Sachiel, as the ruler of this force, does not attend to selfish or immediate desires—his response is slow, robust, and proportional to the operator's ethical intention.

Fundamental characteristics of Jupiterian rites:
- Amplification of results—operations initiated on this day tend to expand, reaching a larger number of people or influences
- Strengthening of spiritual dignity—ideal for those who wish to assume or reaffirm a leadership role in groups, temples, or initiatic communities
- Opening of just paths—the forces of Sachiel favor legal decisions, conciliations, and contractual adjustments
- Activation of gratitude as magnetism—acts of recognition and generosity on this day open invisible doors of abundance

The operator who invokes Sachiel should cultivate greatness of spirit, moderation in requests, and nobility in intentions. It is a day to offer something to the world, not just to ask. Consecrated foods, symbolic donations, or public vows of spiritual service are potent ways to align with his presence.

Practical suggestions for Thursday:
- Wear robes in royal blue, purple, or gold
- Decorate the altar with objects that represent expansion, wisdom, or royalty (books, coins, ceremonial swords)
- Use warm and enveloping perfumes like cinnamon and nutmeg
- Keep the environment in order, with an elegant and welcoming arrangement

His ministers—Asaliah, Nadiel, and Velel—act as administrators of divine graces. Asaliah promotes ethical discernment; Nadiel supervises processes of spiritual justice; and Velel regulates the flow of just generosity, assisting in the harmonious redistribution of spiritual and material resources.

Sachiel is also called upon in moments of institutional crisis, when it is necessary to restore the balance between authority and service, power and humility. He inspires just rulers and protects those who exercise leadership with wisdom and compassion.
- Suggested Psalm: Psalm 112 — "Blessed is the man who fears the LORD, who delights greatly in His commandments..."

FRIDAY — ARCHANGEL ANAEL
- Planet: Venus
- Functions: Love, union, beauty, reconciliation
- Associated Colors: Pink, white, light green
- Perfumes: Rose, jasmine, musk

- Ministers: Donquel, Arquel, Tubiel

Anael is the messenger of universal love and divine harmony. On Friday, his presence envelops the ritual space with gentleness, beauty, and affective magnetism. This is the ideal day for:

- Consecrating relationships and loving alliances
- Performing rituals of affective healing and emotional forgiveness
- Working on self-love and internal reconciliation
- Invoking blessings upon aesthetics, art, and the sensitive expression of the soul

The Venusian influence manifests with sweetness, yet with firmness. Love under Anael is not merely sentimental: it is a restorative force that unites scattered fragments of the self and reverses patterns of rejection or self-punishment. Anael is the angelic artist who shapes the soul according to its original beauty—not as an ornament, but as an authentic expression of its essence.

Striking characteristics of Venusian rites:

- Pacification of affective bonds—Anael favors deep reconciliations, based on empathy and mutual recognition
- Flowering of spiritual self-esteem—excellent for practices that reactivate self-love and heal narcissistic wounds
- Consecration of beauty as divine expression—propitious for work with sacred art, the body as a temple, and refined sensitivity

- Relational magnetism—potentiates the auric field, making the operator more receptive and welcoming in their interactions

Anael asks that the rite be conducted with tenderness and high intention. This is not a day for affective manipulations or selfish passionate requests, but for sincere offerings of love and integration. The aesthetics of the environment matter: fresh flowers, soft candles, and symbols of union are recommended.

Practical suggestions for Friday:
- Wear robes in shades of pink, white, or light green
- Adorn the altar with flowers, rose quartz crystals, and images that evoke divine love
- Use floral perfumes like jasmine or rose essence
- Meditate on forgiveness as an alchemical force and on love as a bridge between worlds

His ministers—Donquel, Arquel, and Tubiel—sustain the more subtle and refined aspects of Anael's action. Donquel works on the harmonization of couples; Arquel facilitates loving and sincere communication; Tubiel works on healing deep emotional wounds, especially those related to abandonment, rejection, or guilt.

Anael is also the patron of spiritual bonds: initiatic friendships, soul relationships, and partnerships consecrated to the common good. He inspires fidelity, tenderness, and aesthetic inspiration—not only in romantic love but also in contemplative life, devotion, and artistic creation.

- Suggested Psalm: Psalm 45 — "You are fairer than the sons of men; grace is poured upon Your lips..."

SATURDAY — ARCHANGEL CASSIEL

- Planet: Saturn
- Functions: Discipline, structure, occult protection, recollection
- Associated Colors: Black, lead, dark blue
- Perfumes: Cypress, black amber
- Ministers: Maiel, Abiel, Urzla

Cassiel is the guardian of thresholds, the angel who watches over the mysteries of time and the silent maturation of the spirit. The vibration of Saturday is austere, introspective, and profoundly contemplative, favoring works of closure, rituals of sealing, and inner reconstruction. This is the ideal day for:

- Rituals of advanced spiritual protection and shielding
- Closure of karmic cycles and pacts that have fulfilled their role
- Work with spiritual inheritances, ancestors, and long memories
- Consecration of legacy objects, such as grimoires, swords, or sacred jewelry

Cassiel does not reveal himself with a bang, but with a dense silence. His energy, ruled by Saturn, imposes containment and gravity. He teaches the operator to deal with limits—of time, of the body, of choices—as portals of wisdom and not as prisons. Under his tutelage, one learns the importance of a slow rhythm, deep patience, and fertile recollection.

Essential characteristics of Saturnine rites:
- An environment of recollection and seriousness—the external silence should reflect the inner listening
- Conscious closures—propitious for concluding processes, dissolving bonds, and sealing spaces
- Strengthening of psychic structures—works to restore boundaries, identity, and energetic sovereignty
- Contact with ancestry—practices of honoring the dead, lineages, and spiritual inheritances

Cassiel rules creative solitude and time as an instrument of transmutation. He does not attend to hasty pleas or superficial invocations. He requires introspection, sincerity, and a willingness to face what is avoided from the operator. His vibrational field is dense, but incredibly transformative when accessed with respect.

Practical suggestions for Saturday:
- Wear dark robes or shades of lead, dark blue, or black
- Light dark-colored candles and use perfumes like black amber or cypress
- Keep the environment sober, with low lighting and a contemplative atmosphere
- Include symbols of Saturn, such as the scythe, the hourglass, or the cube

His ministers—Maiel, Abiel, and Urzla—collaborate in stabilizing the magical field, gathering scattered forces, and sedimenting the acquired learning. Maiel acts on discipline; Abiel protects the energetic portals during the rite; and Urzla guards the accesses of spiritual time, regulating the moments of revelation or concealment.

Cassiel also rules silent initiations, those that do not occur in public rituals but in the solitude of the heart. He is present in the dark nights of the soul, offering a kind of protection that does not prevent pain but gives it form, making it an instrument of alchemy. It is under his aegis that the operator learns to become their own master, capable of recognizing the truth without adornments.

- Suggested Psalm: Psalm 90 — "Lord, You have been our dwelling place in all generations..."
- Important Considerations
- Never mix archangels from different days in a single operation. Each day possesses a distinct spiritual vibration and an exclusive field of action. The overlapping of celestial forces can generate energetic noise, symbolic confusion, and even ritual blockages. The integrity of each rite depends on the purity of the invocation and fidelity to the corresponding temporal flow.
- Always prepare in advance. The success of the magical work is directly linked to the quality of the preparation. This includes crafting or reviewing the seals the day before, organizing the liturgical instruments according to the ruling planet, memorizing or rehearsing the prayers, and aligning the inner intention. Preparation is not bureaucracy; it is consecration.

- The composition of the circle must reflect the exact celestial order. Correctly inscribe the names of the spirits of the hour, the archangel of the day, the king of the air, and the associated ministers. This establishes the sacred geometry necessary for the entry of the spiritual intelligences. Negligence on this point can compromise the effectiveness of the evocation.
- Consecrate your instruments according to the ruler of the day. This not only strengthens the connection with the planetary spheres but also creates lasting spiritual bonds between the operator and their tools. A sword consecrated to the Sun will always carry the light of Michael; a censer consecrated to the Moon will hold the sensitivity of Gabriel.
- Observe the subtle signs before and after each operation. Often, the angels respond through dreams, premonitions, or small changes in the environment. The attentive operator reads these manifestations as confirmations, warnings, or complements to the rite. Spirituality communicates in layers, and fine listening is an essential part of the path.
- Respect the ritual silence after the closing. Avoid immediate distraction. Keep the psychic field collected, without useless conversations, digital exposure, or sensory intoxication. This post-ritual recollection is the space where the seeds that were sown can sprout.

With this chapter, the operator acquires not just a mystical calendar, but an angelic compass that will guide every step in the temple and in life. Each day is now revealed as a living portal, each archangel as a silent master, and each evocation as an encounter between worlds.

Chapter 9
Magical Hours and Seasons

For the practitioner of the *Heptameron*, time is not just duration: it is quality. Every moment carries a specific vibration, determined by the rotation of the stars, the seasons of the year, and the invisible cycles that order the universe. Understanding the magical hours and seasons is not an esoteric curiosity—it is a fundamental requirement of the system. This is because, in the tradition of the *Heptameron*, each rite is a precise conversation with celestial intelligences that move according to their own rhythms. The success of the operation depends, in large part, on holding this meeting at the exact moment when such intelligences are awake, attentive, and inclined to collaboration.

The planetary hours, for example, are not just ancient conventions: they are windows of vibrational access, flows of energy that open and close with a precision that mirrors celestial harmony. By aligning with these hours, the operator is not merely obeying a rule—they are attuning their action to the silent music that governs the movement of the spheres. This attunement confers potency, clarity, and elegance to the rite, like a candle lit at the instant the wind blows in its favor.

The same applies to the magical seasons. It is not enough to know that it is spring or winter from a meteorological point of view. The magician must feel the energetic inflection of the season, perceive how the inner world responds to the changes in light, temperature, and the rhythm of nature. Spring is not just a time of flowers: it is the moment when creative impulses emerge with force, when ideas dormant in winter take shape and direction. To ignore this vibrational quality and insist on working with themes of closure and withdrawal in the season of rebirth can generate friction, a dispersion of forces, and results that fall short of expectations.

Each element of magical time carries its own intelligence, almost as if they were spirits of time. The operator who dedicates themselves to the study of the hours and seasons begins to perceive patterns, to anticipate energetic trends, to prepare in advance for moments of greatest potency. This wisdom of time is silent and requires attention, but it rewards with precision and beauty. Over time, the practitioner develops a kind of inner listening—an ability to perceive the right moment as one feels the shift in the wind before a storm.

This listening is an essential part of the magic of the *Heptameron*. The ancient texts speak of preparing oneself "according to the virtue of the day and the hour," which implies not only a technical adjustment but a state of consciousness attuned to the celestial clock. The magician learns, little by little, to live within another time—a sacred time, where every instant has weight, a name, and a direction. A time that does not run, but breathes; that is not measured, but perceived.

This perception profoundly alters the practitioner's relationship with the world. Monday ceases to be just the beginning of the week: it becomes the day of Gabriel, lord of the waters and lunar mysteries. The ninth hour of a Saturday comes to be perceived as the hour of Mars, intense, cutting, propitious for ruptures or radical cleansings. Summer, with its high light and exposed fruits, invites works of manifestation, while winter, silent and deep, favors dives into the shadow and contact with the dead.

With time, the magician begins to act not according to external urgency, but according to the cadence of the spheres. They learn to wait for the right hour, even if desire burns. They learn to renounce haste in the name of exactitude. For they understand that each planetary hour, each season, and each sign brings a specific key—and that to force the lock when the key has not yet arrived is to waste power and sacrifice harmony.

Therefore, in the *Heptameron,* consulting the time is part of the rite. Observing the sky, checking the planetary hour, recognizing the season, and noting the sign are gestures that attune the operator to the universe. They are, in themselves, devotional acts. Like one who listens to the clock of the heavens not to control, but to participate. Because to operate within the right time is not just to ensure efficacy: it is to become part of the divine movement that unites Earth and Heaven, body and spirit, instant and eternity.

- The Nature of Time in the Heptameron

The Nature of Time in the *Heptameron* goes beyond an abstract ordering of successive moments: it is the very hidden structure upon which magical practice is anchored. Time, in this context, is a living tapestry, interwoven with invisible threads that connect what is above to what is below. Each segment of this tapestry—day, hour, season—pulses with its own intelligence, as if it were an organ of the cosmic body. To understand this structure is more than a technical requirement: it is an act of reverence for the sacred order that sustains the operation.

In the spiritual universe described by the *Heptameron*, time does not advance in a straight line. It moves in spirals, in cycles of opening and closing that reflect the rhythm of the planets, the seasons, and the inner processes of the operator themself. Each return is not a repetition, but a deepening. Today's Monday is not the same as last week's: it brings with it a new tone, a new note in the melody of time, determined by the celestial conditions of that specific moment.

This cyclical conception is not merely poetic—it has practical implications. By knowing that each day of the week belongs to a planet and an archangel, the magician recognizes that they are dealing with a living and specialized presence. Jupiter, for example, does not manifest in the same way as Mars. Their qualities, intentions, and possibilities are distinct. To work on a Thursday without considering the influence of Jupiter is like building a bridge without observing the river's current. There may be technical soundness, but harmony with the flow of time will be lacking.

Furthermore, each hour of the day is under the regency of a specific celestial intelligence. These intelligences are like guardians of temporal portals: they open and close access according to the order of the heavens. To ignore this rulership is, in practice, to try to enter a temple when the doors are sealed. One can force entry, but what is found inside is confusion, echo, an absence of response. Magical time, when respected, responds with synchronicity, clarity, and potency. When ignored, it returns silence, distortion, and fruitless effort.

The analogy with agriculture is particularly fertile: no one plants in winter expecting flowers in spring. Each season requires a corresponding action, and the appropriate time multiplies the results with less effort. So it is with magic. To work "out of time" is like sowing on frozen ground—there may be intention and dedication, but the soil is simply not receptive. On the other hand, a small gesture performed at the right time can have disproportionate effects, like a word spoken at the exact moment that transforms the destiny of a relationship.

In the *Heptameron*, this temporal wisdom is not left to chance. It is encoded in tables, names, planetary sequences, and angelic correspondences that, when properly understood, reveal the secret map of the operation. The operator who learns to decipher this map not only increases their effectiveness—they align themselves with the intelligence of the cosmos. This alignment is, in itself, a form of initiation: it teaches patience, listening, and presence. It teaches that power lies not in mastering time, but in listening to it.

Thus, time in the *Heptameron* is not a backdrop where magic happens: it is an active participant, an ally or an obstacle, depending on how it is treated. To respect it is to honor the invisible laws that govern the subtle worlds. It is to recognize that every fruit has its time of ripening, and that to harvest before the time is right can compromise the flavor, the nutrition, and even the future seed. To work in consonance with time is to transform the rite into a dance, not a contest. It is to make the magical operation an act of communion with the cosmic symphony that pulses in every instant.

- The Planetary Hours

Each day of the week contains 24 planetary hours, which do not correspond to modern clock hours. They are calculated from sunrise and sunset, dividing the daytime period and the nighttime period into 12 equal parts, regardless of their duration in minutes. Thus:
- The 12 hours of the day run from sunrise to sunset;
- The 12 hours of the night run from sunset to the next day's sunrise.

This system reflects an ancient and profoundly spiritual understanding of time: real, living solar time, shaped by the Earth's rotation and the direct relationship with daylight. It requires the practitioner to pay constant attention to nature and local cycles, as each location has its own sunrise and sunset times, influenced by the season and latitude. It is not a time manufactured by gears and conventions, but a natural, organic time, sensitive to the tides of the heavens.

To calculate these planetary hours accurately, the operator should follow these steps:
1. Consult the exact sunrise and sunset times for your location. This information can be obtained from astronomical almanacs, specialized applications, or direct and systematic observation.
2. Subtract the sunrise time from the sunset time to get the total duration of the day. If, for example, the sun rises at 6:00 AM and sets at 6:00 PM, we have 12 hours of light.
3. Divide this value by 12—the result will be the length of each diurnal planetary hour. In the example above, each planetary hour would be exactly 60 minutes, but this only happens on the equinoxes. At other times, this duration varies: in summer, the daylight hours lengthen and the night hours contract; in winter, the opposite occurs.
4. Repeat the process for the nighttime period, from sunset to the next day's sunrise, thus obtaining the 12 planetary hours of the night.

This method creates a fluid time, where the hours do not have a fixed length but respond to the dynamism of light. On some summer days, a planetary hour might be 70 minutes long; in winter, it might be only 50. This makes the time of the *Heptameron* a continuous experience of attunement with nature and a break from the artificial rigidity of clock hands. The operator's consciousness must expand beyond mechanical regularity and enter the living dance of the cosmos.

Modern practice facilitates this process with the use of digital tools. There are reliable applications and websites that automatically provide the planetary hours for each day, in each city, based on astronomical data. However, many practitioners prefer to perform the calculations manually, as a way to engage more deeply with the rhythm of the sky and develop a more acute inner sense of sacred time.

It is important to highlight that the planetary day begins at sunrise, not at midnight as in the civil calendar. This means that, for the *Heptameron*, a Monday only truly begins at dawn, when the first hour is ruled by the Moon. Thus, performing a Monday ritual at 3:00 AM is still, technically, within the planetary Sunday, as the first hour of Monday only occurs with the first ray of sunlight. This distinction is fundamental to avoid errors in energetic synchronization.

Each hour is like a spiritual tide that rises and falls, bringing certain forces to the surface and covering others. By knowing exactly which current is traversing time at that moment, the operator can adjust their sail and rudder, navigating with more precision and less resistance. To ignore this flow is like rowing against the ocean, wasting energy and compromising the fate of the magical vessel. Therefore, attention to planetary hours is one of the most solid practical foundations of the Heptameronic tradition—an exercise in precision, listening, and humility before the celestial order.

- Order of the Planets in the Hours

The sequence of the planetary hours obeys an ancestral logic known as the "Chaldean order," which reflects the apparent speed of the planets in the sky as seen from Earth, from slowest to fastest:

Saturn → Jupiter → Mars → Sun → Venus → Mercury → Moon

This sequence forms the backbone of ritual time in the *Heptameron*. The system works as follows: each day begins with the planetary hour ruled by the planet that gives the day its name. The hours that follow then obey the Chaldean order, restarting the cycle continuously.

For instance, on a Tuesday, which is governed by Mars, the sequence of hours would be:
- 1st Hour: Mars
- 2nd Hour: Sun
- 3rd Hour: Venus
- 4th Hour: Mercury
- 5th Hour: Moon
- 6th Hour: Saturn
- 7th Hour: Jupiter
- 8th Hour: Mars (the cycle restarts) ...and so on for all 24 hours of the day and night.

This structure means that even on a day governed by one primary planetary energy, the operator will find hours influenced by all the others. This multiplicity turns each day into a rich tapestry of possibilities. The magical utility of this system is immense, as it allows the practitioner to:
- Plan rituals with vibrational precision, selecting not only the best day but the most harmonious hour for their purpose.

- Identify favorable windows of opportunity within less auspicious days (for example, using a solar hour for a blessing on a restrictive Saturn-day).
- Avoid energetic dissonances, such as performing a rite of love and union (Venus) during an hour of conflict and rupture (Mars).

Mastering the Chaldean order is, therefore, more than a technical requirement—it is a way of aligning one's inner time with the rhythm of the spheres. It is listening to the celestial rotation as one would a perfect, ancient song. Each planetary hour is a distinct note, and knowing which one to play is what transforms the operator into a true musician of the heavens.

• Practical Applications

• Begin rituals during the planetary hour that corresponds to the archangel being invoked, as this correspondence creates a direct resonance between the operator's call and the vibrational disposition of the celestial spirit. A ritual performed at the right hour finds the door already ajar, facilitating access and communication.

• Avoid initiating operations during planetary hours that contradict your intention. For instance, working with Anael — who governs love and harmony — during Saturn's hour, associated with limitation, melancholy and rigid structure, is like trying to make flowers bloom from stone. The nature of the planets imprints a specific colouring on time, and this colouring may favour or hinder the manifestation of magical intent.

- Use Mercury's hour to consecrate texts, seals and grimoires. Mercury governs language, writing, intelligence and the transmission of occult knowledge. Its hour is especially suitable for inscribing sigils, copying sacred invocations or crafting instruments of spiritual communication.
- Prefer the Sun's hour for illuminations, blessings and protective workings. Solar light, symbolically linked to truth, clarity and vitality, favours operations of inner enlightenment, strengthening the auric field and general consecration. Venus's hour is ideal for rites of union, reconciliation, beauty and affection, being especially potent for restoring loving bonds or attracting virtuous friendships.
- The Angels of the Hours

Each of the 24 planetary hours of the day and night has, in addition to a planetary rulership, a specific angel associated with it. These angels are intelligences that move with the tide of time and manifest spiritual qualities aligned with the dominant planet of that moment. Working with these angels enhances the precision of the rite, as invoking the correct name at the appropriate time creates a direct echo between heaven and the circle.

The Heptameron instructs that, when preparing the magical circle — especially the middle circle — the operator must carefully inscribe:

- The name of the hour (e.g., First, Third, Ninth), indicating its position within that day's planetary cycle;

• The name of the angel of the hour, sourced from reliable angelic tables, which varies according to the planet ruling that specific hour;

• The name of the archangel ruling the day, whose presence guides and sustains the entirety of the rite.

These three names, when properly aligned, form a symbolic trinity that anchors the rite in sacred time. It is as if each operation becomes a letter hand-delivered — at the correct address, date and hour — and the recipient, already awakened, reaches out to receive it. The precision of these names transforms the circle into a living seal of spiritual authenticity, clearly and respectfully recognised in the invisible spheres.

• Structure Example

To clearly illustrate the practical application of these principles, let us consider a detailed example. Suppose the operator wishes to perform a purification and oracular revelation ritual on a Monday, just after sunrise. This choice is not arbitrary: Monday is under the rulership of Gabriel, archangel associated with the Moon, water, and hidden mysteries. The receptive and intuitive nature of this day makes it suitable for introspective practices and symbolic revelation.

Assuming the Sun rises at 6:00 a.m., the first planetary hour begins at that moment and is ruled by the Moon. The second planetary hour, starting just after, will be ruled by Saturn — a planet linked to structure, discipline and deep time. Choosing this hour may seem paradoxical, since Saturn is a slower and denser force. However, this density may be precisely what provides grounding for the oracular work, preventing it from dissipating into fantasy and keeping it rooted in silent, mature listening.

Thus, when preparing the magical circle, the operator must accurately inscribe the corresponding temporal elements:

- Day: Monday
- Archangel: Gabriel
- Hour: Second hour (ruled by Saturn, in this example)
- Angel of the hour: specific name corresponding to Saturn, sourced from traditional tables — e.g., Cassiel, if following a common Kabbalistic line.

Furthermore, as this operation takes place in the winter season (assuming June in the Southern Hemisphere, aligning with today's date), the middle circle should also contain:

- Name of the season: Winter
- Head of the current sign: e.g., Cancer, if the Sun is in this sign (the Sun enters Cancer around 20 or 21 June)
- Symbolic names of the Earth, Sun and Moon for winter: Ignis, Shemesh, Lunastra.

Each of these inscriptions acts as a vibrational seal harmonising the operation with cosmic time. The name of the hour evokes the exact moment, the angel of the hour establishes the communication channel, the archangel of the day consecrates the overarching intent. The seasonal names, in turn, call forth the archetypal qualities of Earth, Sun and Moon in that cycle of the year.

This attention to temporal detail is not merely ornamental — it shapes the invisible field in which the rite unfolds. By operating with precision, the magician becomes a craftsman of time, someone who recognises that every spiritual door has its unique lock, and that each lock responds to a precise combination of names, hours and seasons. It is this combination that transforms the ritual gesture into a bridge between worlds.

• The Signs and Zodiacal Heads

In addition to the seasons, the Heptameron refers to the "head of the sign that governs the season." This is an astrological correspondence related to the tropical zodiac:

- Spring: Aries, Taurus, Gemini
- Summer: Cancer, Leo, Virgo
- Autumn: Libra, Scorpio, Sagittarius
- Winter: Capricorn, Aquarius, Pisces

These triplicities are not just temporal groupings but living expressions of the spiritual quality that pervades each quarter. The "head" of the sign — that is, the sign that opens the season — imprints its dominant force on the ensuing cycle, like a fundamental tone resonating through its subsequent modulations. Aries, initiating spring, bursts forth with vital impulse, announcing movement, rupture with stagnation and the opening of paths. Cancer, at the start of summer, establishes a protective and nurturing field; Libra balances the scales in autumn; Capricorn lays the foundations in winter.

Within each season, the current sign — the one under which the Sun transits at the time of the rite —

can and should be recorded in the middle circle. This annotation is not a secondary detail but a powerful interpretive key. It allows the operator to tailor the operation to the symbolism and rulership of that celestial configuration. For example:
- In Leo: favours works of leadership, strength and public presence.
- In Pisces: favours intuition, dreams, devotional practices.

The sign activates specific layers of the psyche, and its energy modulates both the intention and the result of the operation. In Gemini, communication can be addressed with more lightness and agility; in Scorpio, introspection gains depth and intensity. Thus, integrating the current sign into the ritual provides symbolic precision, attuning the magical gesture to the celestial language of that moment.

- Names of the Earth, Sun and Moon

The Heptameron instructs that the symbolic names of the Earth, Sun and Moon corresponding to the season be inscribed within the circle. These names are drawn from Kabbalistic and Hermetic traditions and do not have literal translations or direct correspondences with profane languages. They are vibrational keys, sonic seals that encapsulate the hidden qualities of the elements they name.

- Example (possible variations):
- Spring:
- Earth: Auria
- Sun: Sorat
- Moon: Levana

- Summer:
- Earth: Ignis
- Sun: Shemesh
- Moon: Lunastra

When correctly inscribed and invoked, these names function as "vibrational keys" that open the field for the seasonal and astral energies to collaborate with the rite. They are not merely symbolic designations but archetypal formulas — names that summon the hidden powers of nature, aligning the rite with the secret breath of Earth and the heavens.

In rituals performed during autumn, for instance, the names inscribed evoke the forces of harvest and introspection, while in winter they activate the silent wisdom of roots and ancestors. The use of these names transforms the magical circle into a point of convergence between the spheres: the earthly plane is elevated to the celestial, and the celestial anchored into the earthly. Thus, the magical operation does not impose itself upon time but roots itself within it, like a ripe fruit blossoming in its proper season.

- Recommendations for the Practitioner
- Maintain a journal with planetary hours and observed outcomes. This diary should not merely be a list of dates and times, but a mirror of the inner journey. The operator should record not only technical data — such as hour, planet, archangel and season — but also subjective impressions, received signs, subsequent dreams, emotional states, unexpected obstacles or significant synchronicities. Over time, this record

reveals invisible patterns and serves as a personal map of temporal navigation.

• Study the effects of the seasons on your spiritual state. It is not enough to acknowledge that it is autumn on the calendar: one must observe how autumn manifests in the body, dreams, desires and inner rhythm. Each season brings a specific summons. Spring calls for openness; summer for expression; autumn for purification; winter for retreat. The sensitive operator will learn to perceive these inflections not as weather, but as states of the soul.

• Avoid improvisation: plan the hour, day and season of each operation in advance. Spontaneity, when it comes to magical time, can be a mistake disguised as enthusiasm. Careful preparation is a form of reverence. Planning does not hinder intuition — on the contrary, it gives it structure. Choosing the wrong hour out of negligence is like arriving for an audience before the court has opened. The true magician knows that every spirit keeps a schedule, and the heavens do not bow to the whims of haste.

• Treat the consultation of time as a ritual in itself — silent, devotional, like one listening to the clock of the sky. Even before the rite begins, the act of observing sunrise, calculating the hours, identifying the sign and sensing the season should be carried out with the same presence required at the altar. This consultation is, in itself, a form of prayer: a gesture that attunes the mind to the pulse of the spheres. It is in this moment that time ceases to be a backdrop and becomes an interlocutor.

- Integration with the Circles

In the chapter on magical circles, we saw that the middle circle contains the data of time:
- Name of the angel of the hour
- Name of the archangel of the day
- Name of the season
- Head of the zodiacal sign
- Names of the Earth, Sun and Moon

This inscription transforms the circle into a living astrological clock, an altar reflecting the order of the heavens upon the Earth. More than symbolic markings, these names act as vibrational anchors. They tune the ritual space to the cosmic moment, as one might tune an instrument to resonate with a celestial orchestra. When all elements are aligned — the angel of the hour, the archangel of the day, the current season, the sign and the occult names of the stars — the circle ceases to be merely a shape traced on the ground: it becomes a precise intersection between the invisible and the visible, where time, space and spirit converge in a single note. It is in this note that the magical word shall be spoken — and the universe will listen.

This refined knowledge of time transforms the operator into more than an executor of formulas: it makes them a sensitive interlocutor of the universe, someone who reads the signs of the sky with the same reverence as listening to a sacred voice. Each calculation, each inscribed name, each choice of hour and season are not merely technical components but gestures of attunement with a living, intelligent cosmos. Thus, time ceases to be an indifferent backdrop and reveals itself as a silent ally — a dancing partner responding with precision to the attentive magician's presence.

Chapter 10
Preparing the Conjuration Ritual

We have reached the threshold. Thus far, the reader has journeyed through understanding and preparation: from the origin of the *Heptameron* to the meaning of its days, from the consecration of the circle to the blessing of the instruments. Now, all the elements begin to align—and the operator finds themselves ready for the central rite of this grimoire: the conjuration. This chapter, therefore, is not just a technical guide. It is a portal. Here, we integrate body, mind, spirit, time, space, and intention into a spiritual symphony that culminates in the presence of the invisible.

To conjure, in the context of the *Heptameron*, does not simply mean to call: it is to dispose oneself to an encounter that involves risk and revelation. There is no room for automatism. Each invocation is a unique event, born from the precise interweaving of all the factors studied in the previous chapters. The conjuration requires the operator to be whole—intellectually lucid, emotionally centered, energetically pure, and spiritually humble. It is not about forcing the appearance of an invisible being, but about creating the ideal conditions for its presence to reveal itself in a natural, organic, and safe manner.

For this, the operator must understand that the rite does not begin with the pronunciation of the formula, but with the inner disposition. From the moment the decision for the operation is made, time already begins to bend around the intention. Dreams change, signs appear, resistances emerge. All of this is part of the process. The magician learns to read these movements as part of the conjuration itself—for the spirit responds not only to the voice, but to the being that becomes audible through it.

Thus, each stage of preparation studied so far—the calendar, the choice of the hour, the study of the seasons, the consecration of the instruments, the purification of the body and space—are not external prerequisites, but parts of the same ritual body. The conjuration is the heart of this body, but the blood that feeds it comes from the attention to every detail. The silence of the space, the firmness of the circle, the exactness of the names, the brightness of the candle, the aroma of the incense—all compose the vibrational environment that makes contact between worlds possible.

Therefore, this chapter must be read with more than attention: with reverence. It does not just present instructions; it opens a passage. What is described here is a threshold between two states of reality—and crossing it requires presence. The reader who has come this far is no longer a curious onlooker: they are an initiate. And as such, they are ready to pronounce the words that unite heaven and earth, time and eternity, desire and revelation.

- The Importance of Complete Preparation

The ritual of conjuration does not begin with solemn words or dramatic gestures. It begins days before, in the silence of intention. The operator does not improvise. They observe the time, study the angels, purify the body, consecrate the utensils, silence the mind, and clarify the purpose. The conjuration is the apex, but its foundation is broad and deep.

To prepare to conjure is like tuning an instrument before a sacred performance: it is not just about knowing how to play, but about doing so in the right key, at the right time, before the right presence. The magician who respects this preparation understands that the invisible responds to care, devotion, and discipline.

Nothing is secondary. Every detail matters:
- The precise hour—chosen based on the planetary rulership and the corresponding angelic disposition, for it is in this rhythm that the spirit moves;
- The appropriate season—for the vibrational qualities of the time directly influence the type of spiritual presence that manifests;
- The correctly traced circle—because it is not just a symbol, but an energetic anchor that delimits and consecrates the space of the operation;
- The right incense—which acts as an aromatic key, attuning the subtle field and inviting the invisible presence;
- The purified fire—not just lit, but consecrated, representing the spirit, the light, and the divine word that must be kindled in the operator's heart;

- The sacred words memorized or printed with reverence—for each pronounced name has spiritual weight, and its correct vocalization is a vibrational call that echoes in the subtle spheres.

Without this foundation, the ritual is just theater. With it, it becomes an invocation. And more than that: it becomes a pact of listening and presence, a legitimate opening of the veil between worlds. Whoever prepares with truth not only performs the rite—they are transformed by it. For the invisible does not manifest where there is disorder, distraction, or presumption. It makes itself present where it finds a dwelling, attention, and respect.

Complete preparation, therefore, is not just a technical requirement—it is a gesture of spiritual hospitality. It is like preparing the house to receive a sacred guest. And the more intimate this preparation, the more natural the encounter, the deeper the listening, the more real the presence.

- The Ideal Moment

First of all, determine the best day and hour. This choice is not just strategic—it is spiritual. Time, in the *Heptameron*, is not a passive backdrop, but a living field of intelligences that respond with precision to the appropriate call.

- Choose the day ruled by the archangel with whom you wish to work. Each archangel governs a day of the week and manifests distinct qualities. By aligning your operation with this ruler, you ensure a fundamental consonance between the goal of the rite and the spirit that sustains it. Do you desire

healing, wisdom, justice, reconciliation? The answer begins with the calendar.
- Calculate the appropriate planetary hour. The most propitious hours are, in general, the first and the eighth of the day, as the first marks the vibrational beginning of the rulership and the eighth repeats this impulse with a stabilizing force. Use reliable tables or astrological applications to determine these hours with precision, considering your geographical location and the season.
- Observe the moon. The moon acts as a mirror and amplifier of human desires. A new moon favors silent beginnings; a waxing moon, initiatives and constructions; a full moon, manifestations and revelations; a waning moon, banishments, severances, and endings. Conjuring in the wrong phase can generate distortions or silences.
- Consider the season of the year. Each season imparts an archetypal coloring to time: spring is expansion, summer is manifestation, autumn is harvest and introspection, winter is depth and dissolution. When conjuring, inscribe this quality into the rite: it will shape not only what manifests, but how and with what intensity.
- Record everything. Note in your magical diary: the chosen day, the hour, the ruling planet, the moon phase, the season, the solar sign, the astral names. This record is not just a memory—it is a devotional act. To write is to fix in the visible world that which already vibrates in the invisible.

It is also an instrument for future learning, allowing you to recognize patterns, understand responses, and refine your practice.

The ideal moment is not when everything is externally available—it is when you have become internally available. When external time and internal time coincide, the conjuration becomes inevitable, natural, and potent. To choose this moment with reverence is the first sign that one is ready to receive what the invisible has to offer.

- The Sacred Space

The place of conjuration must be isolated, clean, and energetically protected. Ideally:

- A room consecrated exclusively to spiritual work—not an improvised space, but a place that, over time, becomes impregnated with the vibrational memory of the rites, turning into a stable point between the worlds;
- Clean walls, without active electronics—as the excess of electromagnetic noise interferes with the quality of subtle perception;
- Natural ventilation, if possible, but without drafts—so that the elements are present in their purity, without dispersing the sacred aromas and flames;
- Soft lighting or only the light of candles—as excessive artificial light dilutes the presence of mystery;
- A fixed or mobile altar facing east—the direction of the birth of light, the starting point of spiritual manifestation.

Before any ritual drawing, perform a purification of the space. This should be done with patience and full intention, as one prepares a sanctuary for the visit of a real presence. This purification follows four essential steps:
1. Physical cleaning: sweep the floor, organize objects, remove everything that is unnecessary. The spiritual world responds to visible order, and material slovenliness is a vibrational obstacle.
2. Purification with a psalm or mantra: the vibration of the sacred word acts as a consecrating sound. Recite Psalm 51:7 ("*Asperges me, Domine, hyssopo, et mundabor...*") with reverence, or another verse consecrated in your tradition.
3. Fumigation with the consecrated perfumes: prepare the incense corresponding to the angel or archangel to be invoked. The smoke not only cleanses the environment but elevates its frequency, making it receptive to the subtle.
4. Tracing of the circle with chalk, cord, or washable paint: do it with precision, consciousness, and silence. The circle is a threshold: it is not just a boundary, but a specific vibrational field, where the encounter can happen without external interference.

During each of these stages, keep your spirit collected. Listen to the space. Feel the vibrational density change. Know that everything that is visibly accomplished is just a reflection of the invisible. By preparing the place, you prepare yourself. By ordering the environment, you order the internal world. By

tracing the circle, you trace the threshold between the human and the divine.
- The Operator and Their Inner State

On the day before the rite, a partial fast (or eating simply) is recommended, along with sexual abstinence, withdrawal from worldly stimuli, silent meditation, and reading the psalms corresponding to the invoked angel. During this period:
- Visualize the presence of the spiritual intelligence with which you intend to work.
- Reinforce your intention with clarity: what do you wish to know, heal, or transform?
- Sleep early, avoid distractions, and review the complete script of the ritual.

This withdrawal is not a moralistic formality but a vibrational alignment. The body, by abstaining from excesses, attunes to the subtle. The mind, by freeing itself from ordinary noise, becomes receptive. The heart, by silencing itself, hears what cannot be said.

The ritual robe is more than a symbolic adornment—it is an extension of magical consciousness. The operator should wear the consecrated tunic, preferably white (a symbol of purity and light) or black with gold or purple details (representing power, wisdom, and spiritual royalty), according to the adopted tradition. This garment separates the profane from the sacred and informs the invisible worlds that this body no longer operates as an ordinary individual, but as a representative of the higher will.

On the belt, one may carry the pentacle, the sigil of the angel, and the printed prayers—not as accessories, but as focuses of presence. Each symbol carries a spiritual memory, a bridge between the name and the one named.

The feet should be bare—as a sign of humility and direct connection with the consecrated ground—or shod in ritualistic sandals that have not been used for other purposes. The head, if possible, should be covered with a light veil or hood, as the veil represents the mystery that is revealed only to the heart that bows.

None of this is superstition. All of this is language. And the invisible listens. The way the operator presents themself to the rite reveals the seriousness with which they treat the encounter. One must remember: you do not go to meet the sacred in a hurry, nor with vanity. Every gesture, every silence, every choice is a note in the symphony one is about to conduct. And the spirit, like an attentive musician, only joins in when it feels that the music has already begun within the invoker's heart.

- Disposition of the Elements in the Space

The organization of the ritual space is not arbitrary. Each object has a precise place, each position carries a meaning. The circle, as a reflection of the cosmic order, demands symmetry, balance, and intention.

Inside the circle:
- The operator—at the center, as the axis between heaven and earth. Their posture should be firm, yet receptive. They do not command: they listen, invoke, align.

- The book with the psalms and conjurations—placed within reach, preferably on a clean stand or portable altar. It should not touch the ground.
- The consecrated wand or staff—to the operator's right, representing the active direction of the will, the channeler of intention.
- A censer with the exorcised fire—to the left, for there burns the element that purifies, elevates, and invites. The incense should be relit whenever necessary, maintaining a continuous aromatic flow.
- The perfumes—arranged in order and named according to their function. They should be identified, in consecrated containers, and handled with parsimony.
- The lamp or ritualistic candle—at the frontal point of the circle, facing east, for there the light of the spirit is born. This flame should not be extinguished before the complete closing of the rite.

Outside the circle:
- The names of the angels of the air at the four corners—these must be positioned with precision: Oriens (east), Paymon (west), Egyn (north), Amaymon (south). The supports can be white cloths, consecrated papers, or discreet inscriptions on the floor.
- The pentagrams at the four angles—protecting the limits of the circle, functioning as vibrational seals against interference. They should be turned outwards, with the top point facing the sky, and

their lines made with ink, chalk, or engraved on fixed supports.

In the middle circle:
- Name of the hour—written in the adopted ritualistic language (Latin, Hebrew, or Greek), with clear and firm calligraphy.
- Name of the angel of the hour—inscribed next to or below the name of the hour, invoking its vibrational quality at the chosen time.
- Name of the archangel of the day—placed in the quadrant corresponding to its rulership, visually highlighted.
- Name of the season—can be inscribed on the floor or intoned before the start of the invocation, contextualizing the rite in the temporal landscape.
- Zodiacal head—the sign in effect at the time of the rite, an archetypal symbol of the energies permeating the heavens.
- Names of the Earth, Sun, and Moon—these should be in harmony with the others and be positioned at the appropriate cardinal points: Earth at the center, Sun to the east, Moon to the west.

This data should be inscribed with consecrated ink, using a ritualistic quill or fine brush, or else intoned with precision and reverence during the tracing of the circle. The most important thing is not the graphic beauty, but the full consciousness when writing them. Each name is a seal, each word is a portal. By inscribing them, the operator anchors the heavens on earth and transforms the space into a vibrant mirror of the celestial spheres.

- Silence and Opening

With everything arranged, light the main candle and make a silent prayer. This moment is crucial: you are about to open a field between worlds. Maintain focus, breathe deeply, do not force visualizations. Just be present.

Silence, here, is not the absence of sound, but absolute presence. It is the veil before the name, the womb of the word. To be in silence is to become a receptive space, to allow the spirit to speak not to the words, but to the core of one's being. During these initial moments, nothing should be rushed. Look around. Acknowledge what has been erected. Acknowledge yourself as the one who erected it.

Next, approach the center of the circle and, with a collected heart, pronounce:

"In the name of the Most High, I open this space with reverence, so that the messengers of Light may make themselves heard, and that no obscure force may penetrate here. So be it."

This initial declaration is more than an invocation: it is a vibrational delimitation. With it, the operator establishes that the conjuration will occur within a pact of light, under a higher authority, excluding any interference that does not belong to the scope of the operation.

- Recommended Practical Sequence
1. Opening of the ritual: maintain a few minutes of silence, standing or kneeling inside the circle,

with eyes half-closed. Breathe with consciousness. Feel the body as part of the space and the space as part of the body. Make a spontaneous or liturgical prayer that invokes protection, clarity, and humility.
2. Lighting of the incense: use the consecrated formula learned during the purification practices. The flame should be lit with reverence, and the censer positioned so that the smoke ascends freely. Visualize the spiral of the aroma as a bridge between the planes.
3. Aspersion of the circle: with a sprig of hyssop or another consecrated instrument, dip it into the lustral water and trace the perimeter of the circle with the gesture of sprinkling. While doing so, repeat the verse from Psalm 51: "*Asperges me, Domine, hyssopo, et mundabor: lavabis me, et super nivem dealbabor.*" Do it with a firm but serene voice.
4. Lighting of the lamp: use the exorcised fire to light the ritual lamp or central candle. This light represents the divine spark, the awakened consciousness at the heart of the rite.
5. Declaration of intent: turn to the center and state clearly, in an audible voice, the purpose of the operation. Say what you seek with the conjuration—healing, guidance, revelation. Do not ask, proclaim. The spirit responds to clarity, not to hesitation.
6. Reading of the appropriate psalm: with the book already arranged, read with precise diction the

psalm corresponding to the ruling archangel of the day. The voice should be used as an instrument, each word launched with full intention.
7. Intoning of the angel's name: pronounce, three times, the name of the angel of the hour, in the respiratory rhythm of your concentration. It can be sung in a monotone, vibrated in a whisper, or intoned with ceremonial modulation.
8. Recitation of the primary conjuration: this is the formal prayer of invocation, usually taken from the *Heptameron* itself. Read it or recite it from memory with all the presence and command you can muster. At this moment, you are officially establishing contact.

At this moment, observe.

Signs may be subtle: a change in the air, warmth, a sudden aroma, a sensation of presence. Remain calm, do not interrupt the sequence. Visible manifestation does not always occur as the imagination expects—but the spiritual presence makes itself known in other ways.

Listening is the true key. The spirit, once summoned in harmony, responds in its own language. It is up to the operator not to seek forms, but to allow themselves to be touched by meanings. To remain in this state is to keep the portal open—with respect, vigilance, and trust.

- Recording and Closing
  After the conjuration:
- Thank the angelic presence, even if you did not perceive clear signs.
- Make a closing prayer (e.g., Psalm 91).

- Ask for protection and withdraw from the circle only after extinguishing the fire, gathering the instruments, and symbolically undoing the tracing.
- Write in the magical diary:
  - Day, hour, and date;
  - Sensations perceived;
  - Errors or distractions that occurred;
  - Inspirations or messages received.

This diary will be your mirror and map in future operations.

The post-ritual moment is not a simple technical conclusion: it is a sacred stage in itself. To close the ritual correctly is as vital as to begin it with purity, for the field opened between worlds needs to be dissolved with the same reverence with which it was raised. Thanking the presence, even if subtle or imperceptible, is a gesture of spiritual humility—for the ordinary senses do not always capture the totality of what has been visited. Gratitude expressed in words or silence seals the pact of respect and prepares the spirit for departure.

The final prayer, like Psalm 91, acts as a vibrational mantle. Its words clothe the operator and the space with a frequency of protection and recollection. It is as if the universe hears a vibrational "amen" that gathers the scattered waves and shields the operator from the echoes that may still resonate in the subtle layers. One should not abandon the circle abruptly. Each candle must be extinguished with intention, each instrument gathered with delicacy. The remaining purification water can be poured onto the earth as a final offering. The tracing of the circle should be undone with the same care with which it was created, walking in the reverse direction, with a gesture that informs the invisible that the portal has been closed. This symbolic undoing does not break the sacred—it accommodates it back into the invisible.

The magical diary, in turn, is not a literary whim, but an initiatic instrument. Writing what was experienced—soberly, without exaggeration or distrust—allows the rite to remain alive in time. Recording the sensations, the possible flaws, the perceived messages, or even the silences carries an alchemical value: it transforms experience into knowledge. Often, the revelation does not occur at the moment of the rite, but in the echo it produces in the following days. A dream, a synchronicity, a sudden memory can be delayed responses to the conjuration. And without the record, these signs dissipate like smoke.

By noting everything with honesty, the magician approaches themself as one who listens to an internal oracle. Over time, these records form a personal cartography of the invisible—they show patterns, reveal tendencies, indicate subtle changes in sensitivity. They are living maps of a spiritual journey that is measured not only by what is seen, but by what is transformed.

If during the rite there were distractions, forgetfulness, or emotional imbalances, they should be described without judgment. The diary is not a courtroom, but a mirror. It is in this honest reflection that the operator learns to recognize the points that require more attention or more surrender. Spiritual practice is not made of impeccable performances, but of true presences. And even mistakes, when observed with humility, become discreet teachers.

Finally, the closing does not end when one closes the diary, but when the operator returns to daily life without breaking the subtle thread of consciousness. The experience of the rite reverberates for hours or days. It is natural to feel more sensitive, introspective, or at times, inexplicably touched. One must allow oneself this passage without trying to name it too soon. Upon leaving the ritual space, walk in silence for a few moments, drink water, breathe deeply. Allow the soul to realign with the body, the body to settle back into the world.

To conjure is to open a door. To close is to shut it with reverence. And to write is to remember that this door can be opened again—not by force, but by the path of listening.

- Ethical Recommendations
- Never conjure out of vanity, revenge, or to manipulate others.
- Never repeat a ritual with obsession.
- Do not change the psalms, names, or hours for your own convenience.
- Respect the invisible as you would respect a loved one.

Magical ethics are not a collection of external rules imposed by an authority; they are the natural expression of an awakened consciousness that recognizes its co-authorship in the fabric of reality. To conjure, in the context of the *Heptameron*, is not to exercise power over the invisible, but to enter into an alliance with it. And every alliance is sustained only by fidelity to subtle but non-negotiable principles. Vanity, for example, is a dissonant noise that destabilizes the harmony of the rite. Invoking a spiritual intelligence with the secret desire to show oneself more powerful or wiser than others not only impoverishes the operation but attracts distorted responses, for the called spirit perceives not the word, but the intention.

Obsession also harms the nature of the rite. The *Heptameron* teaches that there is a time for everything—and to repeat a ritual insistently, out of anxiety or impatience, disrespects this rhythm. Such insistence weakens the operator, unbalances the field, and instead of expanding the connection, it narrows it. The invisible responds with delicacy, not with insistence. There is a cycle of listening and reverberation that must be respected. Repetition should come from a legitimate inner call, not from the desire to control the result.

To modify the psalms, names, or hours for personal convenience is another act of ethical deviation. Each element of the ritual was designed to resonate in a specific field of forces, and its arbitrary alteration disfigures this sacred geometry. Tradition is not a prison, but a language. And like any language, it has its internal rules that guarantee the precise transmission of what one wants to communicate. To change these rules willfully is equivalent to distorting the message before even sending it—and, consequently, to closing the channel through which the response could arrive.

To respect the invisible as one respects a loved one is the synthesis of all ritual conduct. This implies care, listening, consent, reverence. It means not only invoking but also welcoming; not only commanding but also thanking; not only speaking but knowing when to be silent. The magician's ethics lie less in their words and more in the way they offer themself to the encounter: with humility, with attention, with truth. The spirit does not demand perfection, but wholeness. And true respect is born when the operator understands that they are in the presence of a real otherness, not a projection.

This chapter marks the passage from study to practice. Thus far, the reader-initiate has prepared with care. Now, the rite begins. May each gesture be made with presence. May each sacred name be uttered with reverence. And may each conjuration be an act of listening, not of imposition.

You are ready. The circle is traced. The fire has been purified. The time is right. And the word can be spoken.

Chapter 11
The Invocation of the Angels

Having carefully prepared the entire ceremonial context—from the magic circles, blessings, tools, and perfumes to the calculation of timings—the operator now finds themself ready to perform the central invocation of the *Heptameron*: to call into presence the angels, intelligences, genii, and spirits of the day and the hour, according to the model described by Pietro d'Abano. This chapter reveals the internal structure of the conjuration proper, the keywords, the sacred names, and the necessary conduct during the manifestation.

This moment is not merely the execution of a spiritual protocol: it is a conscious opening of a channel between worlds, a crossing between the visible and the invisible that only becomes possible through the confluence of innumerable, carefully arranged elements. Each part of the rite—the position of the circles, the intonation of the psalms, the choice of incense, the exact time ruled by the planets—acts as a gear within an invisible mechanism. When all these gears are in harmony, the portal opens.

The operator, at this point, is no longer an ordinary individual, but a mediator between the planes. Their body becomes the axis between heaven and earth, and their words, when uttered, are no longer just sound and air, but vibration charged with intention, capable of breaking the barriers of the dense world. The preparation does not exempt them from reverent awe—on the contrary, it intensifies it—for they know that from this instant on, they are dealing with intelligences whose nature transcends any human language. It is not a matter of domination, but of a sacred convocation, based on vibrational affinity and hierarchical recognition.

The names that will be pronounced carry centuries of accumulated power. Each one—be it El, Elohim, Agla, Adonai, or the Tetragrammaton—vibrates like a note in a cosmic score that spiritual beings recognize as legitimate. By invoking an angel with its correct name, on its specific day and hour, the magician is not just calling: they are responding to a greater synchrony, harmonizing their action with the orbit of divine time. Hence the importance of everything being ready: any gap in the preparation can break the tenuous thread between the worlds.

The ritual atmosphere will already be densified by the invisible presence of the sacred. The air will seem thicker, the silence will have a tangible weight, and even the light in the room may seem slightly altered, as if the space were being reconfigured. It is at this threshold that the invocation rises as the inaugural word of a new reality. The traditional text of the *Heptameron* is not a jumble of phrases, but a meticulous composition of sounds, meanings, and vibrations that mirror the higher spheres.

The number of repetitions—three—is not arbitrary. It corresponds to the three layers of reality where the angels can manifest: the mental (ideas, images, concepts), the astral (emotions, sensations, visions), and the etheric (environmental changes, heat, aromas). Each repetition, with its respective tone, acts as a subtle wave that propagates towards these planes, inviting the presence to descend or reveal itself.

The silence that follows the invocation is, paradoxically, the most eloquent part of the rite. It is in this space unfilled by words that the response can emerge. The operator must resist the temptation to fill this silence with anxious expectation or reasoning. The secret lies in listening with the entire body, with the senses sharpened but calm, like one contemplating the rising of a star. Some manifestations are as subtle as a shiver; others, as overwhelming as thunder. The important thing is to remain receptive, without projecting desires or fears.

If the presence manifests, there is no room for vanity or panic. The operator must remember that they are not before an entity at their disposal, but a luminous being whose participation was granted through vibrational merit and spiritual integrity. All communication that may occur is born from this mutual recognition: that of the magician for the celestial hierarchy, and that of the spirit for the purity of the human intention.

1. The Purpose of the Invocation

The invocation, in the context of the *Heptameron*, is not a generic supplication nor an abstract mystical request. It is a structured ceremonial command, based on the spiritual authority conferred upon the operator who prepares correctly. Its purpose does not lie in a vague desire for contact with the invisible, but in the legitimate summoning of a spiritual intelligence for a precise action, within defined ethical and vibrational limits. This summons must always have one of the following elevated purposes:

2. To obtain elevated spiritual knowledge: This involves receiving instructions, revelations, or intuitions that expand the operator's consciousness regarding spiritual laws, the nature of the higher spheres, or their personal mission. Such knowledge is not theoretical but experiential, transmitted through symbols, visions, or inner words. It is knowledge that transforms, not just informs.

3. To receive divine guidance or inspiration: Often, in moments of decision, doubt, or existential crossing, the invocation serves as a bridge to receive answers, directions, or counsel from higher intelligences. Such guidance does not replace the operator's discernment but illuminates it, shedding light on the path and the invisible risks.

4. To perform healings, liberations, or harmonizations: In this field, the magician acts as a channel for divine force to alleviate suffering, restore balance, and dissolve dense patterns, whether in themselves or in others. But they must do so only with clear permission, deep compassion, and a precise awareness of the limits of their action. The invoked

angel acts as an intermediary of grace, not as a force to be instrumentalized.

5. To act for the benefit of third parties with permission and ethics: Any action aimed at others must be done with direct authorization or, in exceptional cases, by a compassionate invocation that respects free will and the law of return. One must never invoke a spirit to alter situations for one's own benefit or under the illusion of knowing what is best for another.

There are also more internal and subtle purposes that justify the invocation: the strengthening of spiritual discipline, the deepening of the connection with the celestial hierarchy, or the purification of the energy field. In all these cases, what is sought is not a phenomenon, but a real elevation of the vibrational frequency and a more direct communion with the higher worlds.

The presence that is invited into the circle is not a psychological projection nor a harmless archetype, but a real intelligence, endowed with its own consciousness and a defined cosmic function. Its response is proportional to the purity of the intention, the clarity of the request, and the inner maturity of the operator. Therefore, it is fundamental that the purpose of the invocation has been meditated upon, refined, and, ideally, written down before the rite, so that there is no ambiguity or improvisation during the call.

Finally, it is important to remember that the invocation, even if well-executed, may not receive an immediate response if the purpose is inappropriate, rushed, or unnecessary at the time. Silence is also an answer. It is up to the operator to receive it with humility and to understand that the timing of the light is not the timing of the ego. When, however, the purpose is legitimate, clear, and attuned to the higher spheres, the invoked presence comes—not as a spectacle, but as a silent and transformative epiphany.

6. Moment and Prior Silence

The invocation should occur right after the ritual opening and the intonation of the psalms appropriate to the angel of the day and hour. At this stage, all the elements will have already operated an invisible preparation: the incense will have impregnated the space with its aromatic vibration, the divine names will have already been proclaimed with reverence, and the operator themself will have attuned their intention throughout the entire preliminary process. The field will then be energetically saturated, resonating with the invoked celestial order.

At this point, before uttering any additional words, it is recommended to establish a moment of absolute silence. But this is not merely an auditory silence—it is a suspension of all inner activity that is not in perfect harmony with the rite. The operator should assume an erect posture, with their gaze softly fixed on the center of the circle, and breathe deeply and rhythmically, as if anchoring themself on their own axis. Silence, here, is an offering: by silencing the inner and outer world, the magician demonstrates that they are willing to listen to the unspeakable.

This moment of pause serves to align the operator's vibrational field with the higher planes. It is a space of passage, where the density of the everyday dissolves and one enters, through consciousness and breath, into another state of presence. It is in this interval that the soul presents itself, stripped of desire and expectation, ready only to serve. This is not passivity, but active listening—a listening that prepares the space so that the word to be spoken has creative potency.

The ideal duration of this silence is a few minutes—two or three are sufficient, provided they are charged with real presence. During this time, the operator may perceive subtle changes in the environment: a slight thickening of the air, an internal tremor, a growing sense of sacredness. These signs should not be forced or awaited with anxiety. They come when the field is ripe, and they indicate that the invocation can proceed with authenticity.

This prior silence, therefore, is not a technical pause. It is an active part of the invocation. It is the invisible frame that enhances what is to come. The word will only have power if it is preceded by listening. And listening is only possible when the noise of the self ceases. For this reason, this moment must be lived with extreme reverence, as one who is on the verge of something ineffable. For indeed, they are.

7. Invocation Formula

The traditional text of the *Heptameron* presents the following invocation, which can be slightly adapted for clear and conscious pronunciation:

"I invoke you, O sacred spirit, pure intelligence of the Most High, whose name is [NAME OF THE

ANGEL], minister of the Lord of Hosts, who rules this hour under the governance of [NAME OF THE ARCHANGEL OF THE DAY], with your helpers [NAMES OF THE MINISTERS]. By El, Elohim, Agla, Adonai, and by the Unnamable Name, I call you to appear before this circle of light, manifesting your presence with peace, without deceit, without disturbance, and with the truth that comes from the Light."

This formula should not be uttered as a simple reading, but as a vibrational decree. Each word must be intoned with firm intention and full presence, as if reality itself depended on it. Clarity in diction, regularity of rhythm, and the emotional alignment of the operator are crucial for the invocation to have the desired effect.

8. Triple Repetition

Repeat this invocation three times, alternating the tone of voice between low, medium, and high. This tonal variation is not aesthetic, but functional. Each voice frequency resonates with a specific plane:

1. The low tone reaches the mental level, stimulating contact through ideas, symbols, and intellectual perceptions.
2. The medium tone penetrates the astral plane, where emotions, visions, and more fluid intuitions can emerge.
3. The high tone vibrates in the etheric, provoking sensible changes in the physical or sensory environment.

This progression of tones creates a vibrational ladder that favors the descent or manifestation of the invoked spirit. It is fundamental that the operator maintain the same verbal text in all three repetitions, allowing the only variable to be the tone of voice and, secondarily, the degree of emotional energy involved.

9. Three-Minute Pause

Next, maintain silence for three full minutes. During this time:
- Keep your gaze fixed on the center of the circle, the ritual flame, or the consecrated symbol.
- Breathe deeply, in a serene manner, remaining open to whatever may arise.
- Observe any change in the environment: temperature, luminosity, air density.
- Pay attention to sudden intuitions, inner images, silent voices, shivers, or sensations of presence.

The time should be timed with precision. Even if nothing perceptible occurs, these minutes are an integral part of the formula, as they constitute the necessary inner space for the spirit to respond. Haste or anxiety dissolves the field; patience and silence consolidate it.

10. Sigils and Seals

During the invocation, it is recommended that the operator keep in view, on the altar or on a consecrated parchment:
- The sigil of the angel, drawn with precision and previously activated.
- The name of the angel written in Hebrew (or in a sacred transliteration).
- The psalm corresponding to the spirit, prepared in advance.

These elements function as vibrational anchors. The sigil is a visual code that attracts and fixes the presence. The sacred name acts as a key of vibrational identity. The psalm is a verbal channel that resonates with the spiritual function of the entity. Together, these three elements amplify and stabilize the field of manifestation, reducing interference and making the invocation more precise and safe.

All of these should have been anointed with consecrated oil, purified with incense, and previously invoked with appropriate words. Only when ritually charged do these objects pass from symbolic representation to operative tools. The magician must not improvise at this stage—negligence with the symbolic elements results in sterile rituals or, worse, imprecise connections with intelligences that do not correspond to the call.

The conjuration, therefore, is sustained not only by the word but also by signs, forms, names, and silence. Each of these elements is a living part of the formula, and their correct integration determines the degree and quality of the manifestation that will follow.

11. Operator's Behavior

The magician's posture is a fundamental part of the invocation. The body is the channel through which the energy will circulate. Thus, during the invocation:
- Remain standing, firm, with feet together or in an equilateral triangle.
- Avoid excessive gestures, other than those prescribed (such as raising the right hand or making a cross on the chest).

- The tone of voice should be firm and respectful, without shouting or excessive murmuring.
- The gaze should be centered on the middle of the circle, or on the ritual fire.
- Never leave the circle during the invocation, even if you feel fear or ecstasy.

The physical and emotional stability of the operator is the silent axis that sustains the spiritual manifestation. Every gesture, or absence thereof, communicates to the invisible plane the inner disposition of the one who invokes. The body, in this context, ceases to be merely a vehicle of expression and becomes a living temple—both a receptacle and an emitter. The slightest instability, distraction, or hesitation vibrates beyond the form and can compromise the clarity of the call.

During the invocation, the magician must assume a total presence: feet rooted, spine erect, chest open. This bodily posture expresses not only firmness but also confidence and spiritual readiness. The gaze, directed towards the center of the circle or the ritual fire, should remain steady but without tension. The fire, moreover, is more than a symbol: it is a living mirror of the spirit, and fixing one's gaze on it helps to keep the mind anchored and the heart alight.

Inner silence, as much as the vocalized word, is decisive. Any disordered internal dialogue—doubt, fear, expectation, pride—can interfere with the field. Therefore, mental discipline must be cultivated not only at the moment of invocation but from the preliminary preparations. The operator who presents themself before the angelic presence must be whole, clean, focused, and available.

12. Repetition of the Invocation

If after three minutes there is no perceptible manifestation, the invocation can be repeated one or two more times, slightly changing the tone and reinforcing the intention. Use, if you wish, this variation:

"By Melchizedek, by Enoch, by Elijah, righteous servants of the Light, I cry out for your presence, O angelic spirit [NAME], faithful servant of the Most High. Come in peace, respond to my voice, manifest yourself visibly or sensibly in this circle, for your word is called with faith and your presence is invoked with purity."

This repetition should not be done with impatience or frustration, but with even more solemnity. The absence of an immediate manifestation does not mean failure but may reflect the need for a vibrational reinforcement. Repetition is also a form of spiritual persistence, and when done with humility and firmness, it often unblocks resistances or dense layers that delay the response.

The tone of voice can be slightly intensified or softened, depending on the operator's intuition. The important thing is to maintain the purity of the intention, without being overcome by scattered emotions. The act of repeating, in this context, is a ritual gesture of faith and concentration, not of blind insistence. It is a way of reaffirming the spiritual commitment to the light that is being called.

13. During the Manifestation

If a clear sensation of presence arises (wind, aroma, light, cold, sound, form), the operator must maintain composure. Do not interrupt the rite. Follow these principles:

- Breathe deeply, give thanks mentally.
- Wait for energetic stability (avoid premature euphoria).
- Keep your hands open or over your heart.
- Allow the spiritual presence to establish itself.

The manifestation can occur in a subtle or intense manner, and its nature often reflects the operator's sensitivity and the degree of affinity with the called spirit. The important thing is to avoid any hasty reaction. Emotions such as surprise, excitement, or fear should be inwardly welcomed and transmuted into reverence and stability. The magician's serenity is, at this instant, the anchor that allows the spiritual presence to consolidate fully.

The manifestation can be:

1. Mental or visionary: symbolic images, archetypes, silent words, colors, or scenes that form with clarity in the mind, often with immediate spiritual meaning.
2. Auditory or sensory: internal voices, clear words, or whispers perceived without a physical origin; harmonic noises or sonic vibrations; specific bodily sensations like warmth in regions of the body, tingling, or shivers.
3. Environmental or etheric: a change in the density of the air, an alteration of temperature, the

presence of an unidentified aroma, a variation in the ambient light even without a visible external cause.
4. Tangible (rarer): perception of a visible point of light, a shadow with a defined shape, a concentrated breeze, the displacement of a light object, or even a soft and precise tactile sensation.

Each type of manifestation carries with it a distinct energetic quality, and it is the operator's duty to perceive it without projecting expectations or judgments. The angelic presence does not seek to impress, but to communicate, and this communication is almost always modulated so as not to break the magician's emotional integrity.

14. If the Manifestation is Threatening

In very rare cases, the operator may feel discomfort or an oppressive presence. In this case:
1. Do not abruptly interrupt the ritual.
2. Reinforce the divine names: Adonai, El Shaddai, Agla, Tetragrammaton.
3. Make the sign of the cross with your dominant hand.
4. Recite Psalm 91 in a firm voice.

It is essential to understand that the presence of discomfort does not necessarily imply malevolence—it could be an intense force poorly assimilated by the operator's field. However, if the sensation becomes oppressive, confusing, or clearly hostile, the magician must resort without hesitation to the authority of the sacred names.

If the discomfort persists, say:

"In the name of the Most High, if you are not a spirit of light, depart from this consecrated circle. I cast you out by the light of Truth and by the flame of the Spirit."

This proclamation, made with firm faith and clarity of voice, tends to reorder the field immediately. Afterward, the operator should remain in silence, attentive to the re-establishment of vibrational balance. Only when the atmosphere is fully stabilized can the closing prayer be performed, sealing the ritual space with harmony and protection.

15. Observations on the Ethics of Invocation

- Never invoke an angel out of mere curiosity. Curiosity, however legitimate it may seem, is not a valid criterion for contact with spiritual intelligences. The angel is not a spectacle or a phenomenon to be witnessed. It is an elevated consciousness whose presence demands respect and a clear purpose. The invocation must be born from an authentic inner call, not from a craving for extraordinary experience.
- Always have a clear and worthy purpose. The ethical foundation of any rite lies in the intention that sustains it. The operator must know exactly why they are calling, what they are seeking, and on what level they wish to act—whether for their own benefit, for others, or in communion with the divine. Ambiguous, selfish, or immature purposes reverberate in the field and block manifestation.

The clarity of the objective not only guides the rite but also delimits its safety.
- Never demand from or threaten a spiritual entity. The relationship between magician and spirit is one of alliance, not domination. The operator's authority does not authorize them to coerce, command, or threaten the invoked being. Even when faced with a reluctant or silent spirit, the tone must be one of reverent firmness, never of arrogance. The language of the sacred does not admit arrogance. One who tries to impose themselves runs the risk of breaking the vibrational link and attracting distortions or falsifications of the presence.
- Avoid rituals if you are emotionally unstable. The operator's internal state is the true temple of the operation. Fear, anger, intense sadness, or unbalanced euphoria are vibrations that cloud the field and make any contact imprecise or even dangerous. Before starting any spiritual work, it is essential that the magician is centered, pacified, and sober. Emotional stability is a silent offering that purifies the space even before the words are spoken.

In addition to these direct observations, it is necessary to understand that the ethics of invocation are not limited to the ritual moment. They extend to the operator's entire conduct before and after the call. Keeping silent about received experiences, respecting the times of assimilation, not divulging revelations in a vain or commercial manner, and, above all, living in coherence with the principles one seeks to touch: all of this constitutes the true circle of protection.

Ethics also require that the magician knows when to desist if necessary. If, while preparing for the invocation, they perceive doubt about the purpose, mental confusion, energetic imbalance, or a lack of integrity in the intention, it is preferable to postpone the rite. Spiritual time does not follow the logic of human urgency. The operator's maturity is also manifested in the ability to listen to the signs that call for waiting.

The invocation is, ultimately, a spiritual pact. By raising their voice, the magician affirms before the invisible: "I am ready to receive and sustain a presence that transcends me." Such an affirmation requires an inner righteousness that cannot be improvised. That is why the response—when it comes—is not just a manifestation, but a recognition. The spirit responds because it sees, in the circle and in the heart of the operator, the reflection of its own light.

The human voice rises towards the invisible, like a thread of light that wishes to rediscover its origin. It is not just about emitting words—it is the soul that projects itself, whole, in an attempt to touch what lies beyond the veil. When the call is legitimate, the sacred responds. Sometimes, the response comes as a silence charged with presence. Other times, as a sudden vibration that runs down the spine, a light that ignites within, an inaudible word that seems to have always been known. Listening is the true meeting point—not the listening done with the ears, but with the wholeness of one's being.

To be in the presence of the manifestation is to withstand its intensity without becoming scattered, to welcome its delicacy without doubt. It requires the courage to remain in the center of the circle even when the mystery approaches, and the humility to recognize that nothing there was "conquered," but simply granted. The spirit does not descend out of obedience, but out of affinity, and this affinity is born from the purity of the intention, the rigorous preparation, and the sincerity of the call.

When the response reveals itself, even for brief moments, the world is never the same again. The operator has been touched by something that surpasses language and memory. It is not about accumulating experiences, but about allowing oneself to be transformed by them. And if nothing is perceived, still something will have been sown in the silence—for every true invocation leaves a trace, a vestige of light, a subtle realignment that will reveal itself in due time.

The encounter with the angel does not begin when it appears, but when there is a willing heart, a consecrated space, and a worthy purpose. What begins with words ends in presence. And what remains is the bond, the vibration that continues to echo even after the rite is closed.

May your voice be pure, your intention luminous, and may the angels respond to your truth with benevolence.

Chapter 12
Communication and Petition

The invocation of the angels marks the beginning of one of the most sacred stages of the ceremonial process described in the *Heptameron*: the moment of communication. After feeling or perceiving the presence of the evoked spiritual entity—whether subtly or tangibly—the operator must conduct the rite with reverence, clarity of purpose, and discernment. This chapter deals with the art of dialoguing with celestial spirits, formulating petitions, listening with spiritual sensitivity, and adequately recording the messages received.

This communication is not limited to speech or articulated thought but involves a deeper and more subtle kind of listening, an inner openness that allows spiritual reality to manifest without the limitations of common language. The operator must cultivate a state of mind in which the mind is lucid but not hyperactive; receptive, but not anxious. It is about entering into consonance with a higher plane of consciousness, where linear time loses its force and the present moment becomes charged with meaning.

Before any word is spoken, there is a sacred silence that needs to be heard. This silence is often the first means of response from the angels—a silence that communicates more than a thousand phrases, a pause laden with presence, in which the heart intuits that it is being heard and welcomed. Communication, at this level, is more of a communion than an exchange of information. It is the soul speaking with another soul, under the aegis of the sacred.

It is fundamental to understand that the language of angels is symbolic and multisensory. A faint aroma that appears from nowhere, a luminous impression behind closed eyes, a sudden shiver down the back—all of this can be a response. The rational mind may try to ignore these signs, judging them as irrelevant or imaginary. But the trained operator learns to respect these subtleties as legitimate manifestations of the spiritual presence.

When formulating the petition, the tone of voice, even if only mental, must be imbued with reverence and sincerity. The heart must be clean of manipulations or petty desires. What is sought is not an advantage, but an attunement with the greater good. And this completely changes the nature of the request. The uttered phrase may be simple, but if it comes from a deep place in the soul, it reverberates on the subtle plane with force and dignity.

During the listening, patience is an essential virtue. Angels do not operate at a human pace. Sometimes, the answer comes in the same instant; other times, it manifests in dreams in the following days, in chance encounters, in words spoken by strangers. The communication does not end with the closing of the ritual—it unfolds, like a sacred echo, through unexpected paths. The operator must remain attentive, even after the rite, cultivating the inner silence that allows them to recognize these resonances.

There are also moments when the operator feels, with undeniable clarity, that a presence is before them, awaiting the human word. In that instant, time seems suspended. The air acquires an almost palpable density. It is like being before a mirror that sees beyond appearance—a mirror that reflects the most intimate truth. To speak at this moment requires courage, for everything that is false resonates dissonantly. The voice of the human spirit must then rise with authenticity, for the angel recognizes the truth of the heart even before the words.

After the response, gratitude must be immediate and sincere. It seals the communication and honors the established bond. Even if the response is not what was expected, or if there is no perceptible response, the act of giving thanks keeps the channel clean and open for future communications. It is a recognition that something greater has been touched—something that, even if invisible, acts on the plane of the soul.

With time and practice, the operator develops a kind of listening that goes beyond the senses. They learn to discern between their own emotions and the authentic vibrations of the spiritual plane. They learn not to cling to the answers, but to welcome them with humility. They learn, above all, that the true power of communication with angels lies not in obtaining what one wants, but in aligning oneself with the will of the Divine.

- The Consciousness of Presence

Before attempting any form of active communication, the operator must stabilize their own consciousness. This means quieting the mind, balancing the emotions, and consciously anchoring oneself in the body, in order to become receptive to subtle realities. This preparation is not merely technical, but spiritual: it is an internal alignment, in which body, mind, and soul become a single instrument of listening and communion.

The spiritual presence does not always manifest with visual or auditory clarity. In many cases, it is perceived as a field of energy that imperceptibly modifies the atmosphere of the ritual space. This presence can be felt as:

- A distinct vibrational field that envelops the body or the environment;
- An expansion of consciousness, as if time were slowing down and thoughts were becoming sharp;
- A dense quietude, which silences the mind with a silent and enveloping peace;
- A luminous lightness, almost tactile, as if the light acquired a soft texture around the operator.

Common signs of angelic presence:
- Sudden mental clarity;
- An increase in body or environmental temperature;
- A change in the luminosity of the ritual space;
- A light breath of air without an apparent physical cause;

- A sudden intuition with specific information.

These signs should not be interpreted as absolute guarantees of angelic presence, but rather as indications to be welcomed with discernment. The operator must remain centered and receptive, without rushing to conclude or interpret what they are feeling. Spiritual listening is a subtle art, and it requires surrender more than control.

It is essential to understand that each operator has perceptual channels that are more developed than others. Some are more visual, others auditory, and still others are sensitive to emotional or bodily states. None of these forms is superior or inferior: all are valid, as long as they are accompanied by humility and inner attention.

Spiritual communication requires inner listening and surrender to the experience. This listening occurs in the body and soul, and it requires from the operator a state of attention that is, at the same time, relaxed and awake. A good preliminary practice might include breathing exercises, a ritual bath, meditative preparation of the space, and a few minutes of silent contemplation before a lit candle. These are gestures that help to adjust the operator's frequency to the angelic plane.

With time and practice, the operator becomes capable of distinguishing between the authentic movements of the spirit and the agitations of their own ego. By keeping a diary of perceptions, they can record not only the explicit signs but also the more subtle nuances of the presence. With this, their listening matures, they recognize patterns, and they develop a deeper relationship with the invisible worlds.

- The Ethics of the Approach

The moment of communication is not an interview nor a bargain. The celestial spirit is not subject to human will. Therefore, the correct attitude is one of reverence, humility, and clarity of intention. This inner ethic must be rooted even before the beginning of the rite, as it is what sustains the quality of the spiritual interaction. When approaching a being of light, the operator must empty themself of pretensions and assume a posture of sincere listening, like one approaching a mystery greater than they can comprehend.

Some fundamental rules:
- Never formulate selfish, vain, or vengeful requests;
- Never try to force an immediate response;
- Never interrupt the silence with mental chatter or anxiety;
- Always begin with gratitude and praise to the Divine.

These rules are not simple formalities. They exist to protect both the operator and the integrity of the contact. A selfish request contaminates the vibration of the rite and can attract entities not in keeping with the light. The attempt to force answers demonstrates spiritual immaturity and often generates illusions or an echo of one's own desire. The silence must be respected as part of the dialogue—it is in silence that the presence communicates most deeply. And the initial praise is a way of remembering that contact is only possible through divine permission, not by personal merit or control.

A good start can be:

"In the name of the Most High, I thank you for your presence, O spirit of light. I ask that, if it be the Divine Will, you answer me with clarity and truth, for the greater good."

This invocation not only delimits the operator's elevated intention but also creates a vibrational frame that elevates the space of the rite. It is like opening a door with the key of humility, recognizing that all true spiritual dialogue is, above all, an act of grace. In this state of mind, communication becomes more fluid, sharper, and, above all, safer. By establishing this ethic as a foundation, the operator aligns not only with the angels but with the very higher purpose of magical practice: to serve the light with consciousness, truth, and devotion.

- How to Formulate the Petition

A spiritual request should be made on three levels:

1. Clarity of language: Avoid long, ambiguous, or vague sentences. Get straight to the point. Spiritual entities do not operate on assumptions; they respond to what is said with precision. A clear request demonstrates that the operator understands what they truly desire and expresses it without beating around the bush. To this end, it is useful to write the request beforehand and reread it before the rite, adjusting the vocabulary until the words convey the exact intention without exaggeration or omission.

2. Purity of intention: Reflect before the rite: is this just? Will it cause harm to anyone? What is the ultimate purpose? A request born from a desire for control, from emotional neediness, or from vanity loses spiritual force and can compromise the integrity of the contact. One that springs from a sincere heart, from the will to serve the light, or to heal what is misaligned, carries a vibration that naturally aligns with the higher plane. Purity here does not mean perfection, but deep honesty with oneself.
3. Surrender of the outcome: Acknowledge that the answer may not be immediate, or it may come in another form. When making a request, the operator must also let go of a rigid expectation of how and when the answer will come. This demonstrates faith and spiritual maturity. An appropriate way to express this surrender is to say:

"If it is permitted, may I be shown what I need to know or do."

- Examples of Petitions
- "I ask for help to discern the professional path most aligned with my soul."
- "I ask for healing for [name], if this is within divine harmony."
- "I ask for guidance to deal with this fear that blocks me."
- "I ask for a blessing upon this project that I wish to carry out with purity."

These examples are based on a solid ethical and spiritual foundation. They are requests that seek growth, clarity, healing, or alignment with the greater good—not the satisfaction of immediate or superficial personal desires.

Avoid questions like:
- "Am I going to win the lottery?"
- "Will so-and-so leave their partner to be with me?"
- "What is the lucky number?"

Such questions reduce the rite to a common fortune-telling practice, disconnected from the deeper purpose of angelic communication. Furthermore, they demonstrate an intention based on control or desire, which can compromise not only the truthfulness of the response but the very quality of the evoked presence. The wise operator knows that the most valuable answers are those that illuminate the path of the soul, not just the momentary interests of the personality.

- Forms of Response

Spiritual entities respond in different ways, according to the operator's level of development and the nature of the question. The main forms are:

1. Direct intuition: A clear idea arises in the mind, with intuitive certainty. There is no hesitation, no reasoning. It is like a truth planted in the consciousness, which reveals itself completely and with sudden clarity. This type of response is usually accompanied by a sense of relief, as if something very essential had been recognized and welcomed immediately.

2. Mental words: A short phrase echoes internally with force. It is not confused with ordinary thought—it has weight, direction, and a distinct tonality. It often comes in the second person ("do this," "listen better," "trust now") and can sound with a sweet yet firm authority. It is important to record the phrase exactly as it came, without adapting it to personal will.
3. Symbolic images: Visions or archetypes are shown (swords, doors, lights, etc.). This form is more frequent in operators with an active imagination or heightened visual sensitivity. The images should not be interpreted immediately but observed as if they were dreams: symbols that speak to the unconscious and can carry multiple meanings. A door might mean passage, choice, protection, or revelation, depending on the spiritual context of the rite.
4. Physical signs: A candle flickers strongly, the incense smoke moves in an unusual way. Crackling sounds in the environment, the falling of light objects, or a sudden change in the thermal sensation of the space can also occur. These signs, when they coincide with the exact moment of the request or listening, should be recorded with attention. It is the language of the invisible crossing over to the material plane.
5. Significant silence: When there is no response, this is also a response. It may indicate:
    - That the question is inappropriate;
    - That it is not the right time;

- That the answer will come by another means (dream, a later sign, daily intuition).

This silence is not empty. It is dense, alive, as if something were being gestated beyond the reach of the mind. The operator must respect it with reverence, without trying to fill it with suppositions. It is in this interval that the soul learns to trust, to listen to the timing of the sacred, and to recognize that there is wisdom in waiting as well.

- Immediate Recording

Right after receiving the response (or the absence of one), it is essential to write everything down. This simple gesture preserves the purity of the experience and allows the memory of the rite not to be diluted by the daily flow of thoughts. The magical diary is not just a technical record, but an extension of ritual consciousness: a mirror where the operator learns to read their own spiritual trajectory.

- Bodily sensations: Describe if there was warmth, a chill, heaviness, or lightness in the body. In which part did they manifest? How long did they last? Such sensations often coincide with the spiritual presence and can indicate the type of energy involved.
- Mental images: Note down symbols, scenes, colors, faces, landscapes. Even if they seem vague or disconnected at the moment, these elements may acquire meaning days later, in dreams, synchronicities, or subsequent reflections.
- Words or ideas that arose: Record with precision what was heard mentally, without adapting or

correcting it. The language of the spirit can be direct, poetic, symbolic, or paradoxical. The important thing is to keep the original content intact for later evaluation.
- Emotions awakened: Name with clarity what was felt: peace, gratitude, sadness, awe, reverence. Also note the intensity and duration of the emotion. Often, the emotional vibration is the main means of transmitting the message.
- Doubts or certainties that emerged: Finally, write down any feeling of confirmation, discomfort, or doubt that arose. These impressions are part of the response and help to discern between a legitimate communication and internal noise.

This recording can be made in the magical diary, with the date, time, invoked angel, and a detailed description. It is highly recommended that this notation be done immediately after the closing of the rite, before the rational mind interferes with the received content. Over time, this diary becomes a true map for spiritual deepening—revealing patterns, frequencies, recurring themes, and inner transformations. It is what allows the operator to verify the truthfulness of the messages, observe their own evolution, and refine their listening of the sacred with maturity and lucidity.

- Avoid Hasty Interpretations

Not everything that arises in the mind during the ritual is a spiritual response. The subtle plane is delicate, and the operator needs to cultivate a refined discernment to separate what comes from the spirit and what comes from their own psyche. Recurring thoughts, repressed desires, anxieties, or emotional projections can infiltrate the experience, creating noise that, at first glance, sounds like authentic messages.

Therefore, follow this rule:

Every true answer is accompanied by peace.

This peace is not just the absence of conflict, but a vibrational state that calms, expands, and aligns. A true message may even bring a difficult instruction or a call to transformation, but even so, it carries a note of serenity that rests in the soul as a silent confirmation. On the other hand, if there is doubt, insecurity, excessive euphoria, or obsession with the answer, wait. Spiritual excitement can confuse the ego and lead to error—especially when neediness or haste is involved.

Reflect. Meditate days later. Give your consciousness time to settle what was experienced. Write it down, but do not conclude immediately. Mature spiritual practice requires patience, and one of the highest forms of wisdom is knowing how to wait with humility.

A true sign reinforces itself over time. It resurfaces in dreams, synchronicities, repeated intuitions, or unexpected confirmations. A mistake, on the other hand, dissipates with silence. What is not rooted in the spirit tends to dissolve in the face of attentive listening and time. Learning not to cling to the immediate answer is part of the magician's path. For more important than knowing is being ready to receive the truth—even if it dismantles illusions.

- Non-Verbal Communication

Often, beings of light respond without words. Only with presence, vibration, tenderness, calm, or a loving silence. This is also a response. There are requests that do not require instruction, but rather healing, relief, or welcome. In these cases, the angel acts more like a balm than a messenger.

In these instances, the request has been received, and perhaps the blessing is being granted on an invisible level. The operator feels a change in the field, a relief without a logical cause, a sweet emotion, or a softening of internal tensions. There is no phrase, no image—just a silent knowing that something has been touched and transformed.

"Not every answer is an instruction. Some are a silent healing."

The operator must learn to recognize this type of blessing and not be frustrated by the absence of direct words. Non-verbal communication requires a deeper listening, devoid of expectations. It is the space where the soul learns to trust, even when the mind does not yet understand. And this trust, cultivated with constancy, is the true link between the visible and the invisible.

- When the Response is Disturbing

At certain moments, instead of serenity and clarity, the operator may be surprised by an uncomfortable sensation, a threatening vision, or a heavy emotion that darkens the mind and heart. Such occurrences should not be ignored or hastily rationalized as part of the experience. Although the spiritual plane contains vast gradations of light, it is also susceptible to interference, especially when the operator's vibrational field is not yet fully stabilized.

If a negative image, a harsh word, or an oppressive emotion arises, interrupt the contact. This does not mean fear, but spiritual responsibility. Discernment at this moment is vital: the operator must remember that truly luminous entities do not manifest through intimidation, despair, or violence. The vibration of the higher light is constructive, even when incisive—it never confuses, terrifies, or subjugates.

In this case, immediately follow a protocol of protection and closing:

1. Recite the Divine Names: Elohim, El Shaddai, Adonai, Agla. These sacred names evoke high protective frequencies, capable of dissolving dissonant presences and restoring the balance of the ritual space.
2. Make the sign of the cross. This ancestral gesture symbolizes the vertical axis of transcendence and the horizontal axis of incarnation, creating a symbolic shield that reaffirms the alliance with the divine plane.
3. Recite Psalm 23 or 91. Both psalms are recognized as potent spiritual shields. Psalm 23 brings the support of the Divine Shepherd who leads through the shadows with firmness and love. Psalm 91 is a hymn of refuge under the wings of the Most High, invoking direct protection against hidden forces.
4. Dismiss the spirit in peace with firmness and compassion:

"If you are of the light, calm yourself and speak with clarity. If not, in the name of the Most High, depart."

This formula should not be said with anger, but with spiritual authority. It reaffirms the operator's center of light and delimits the field of action.

Remember: a true spirit does not impose itself with fear or violence. Even if its message may be demanding, it is never corrosive. A prepared operator knows this difference by the vibration, more than by the words.

- When the Spirit Responds Clearly

When the spiritual presence manifests in a clear way—whether through internal words, visual symbols, or direct counsel—the operator enters a state of living communication. It is a delicate moment of great potency and should be welcomed with serene concentration.

- Maintain focus and calm. The mind should avoid slipping into enthusiasm or haste. An excess of emotion can cloud the clarity of what is being received.
- Give thanks mentally. This inner gesture strengthens the connection and confirms the respectful character of the encounter. Sincere gratitude acts as both a link and a protection.
- Ask for clarification if something is not understood. Angels are not offended by an honest search for understanding. A simple phrase like "can you show me in another way?" can bring new light to the received content.

- Never interrupt abruptly. Let the communication conclude naturally. When the flow begins to cease, respect this rhythm. Be silent, breathe in, and just observe. Do not try to artificially prolong the contact—just like a precious visit, the spirit departs at the right time.

These moments of clear response are like pearls: rare, precious, formed in the depth of communion. The true operator welcomes them with reverence, without attachment. Because they know that the greater wisdom lies not in multiplying contacts, but in transforming oneself from each one.

- Closing the Communication

After receiving the response, follow this structure:

1. Give sincere thanks:

"I receive your presence with gratitude. May peace accompany you."

This thanksgiving should be more than a formality—it is a conscious recognition that a bridge between worlds has been established, even if for a brief moment. Gratitude seals the space of listening with spiritual dignity, closing it with the same reverence with which it was opened.

2. Be silent for a few seconds.

This silence is not just a pause: it is the moment when the spirit withdraws and the soul assimilates. As at the end of a sacred song, it is in this silent space that the resonance of the encounter echoes internally, allowing consciousness to integrate what was received.

3. Finish with a prayer to the Creator:

"Most High, I thank you for your light and for allowing this sacred encounter. May all be for the good."

The prayer to the Creator not only ends the rite but consecrates it. It is a return of what was received to the divine plane, like one who gives a seed back to the earth after contemplating it in their hands. By making this prayer, the operator affirms that they do not seek to appropriate the experience but to integrate it with humility into their journey.

4. Inhale the incense deeply, acknowledging the end of the contact.

This simple gesture has a profound symbolism: the incense, the element of air transmuted by fire, represents the link between the visible and the invisible. By consciously inhaling it, the operator anchors their presence back on the physical plane, closing the portal opened during the spiritual contact.

Closing the communication with care is as sacred as beginning it. Many operators neglect this moment, immediately seeking to interpret, comment, or act based on the received message. However, it is this conscious closing that preserves the integrity of the rite and protects the psyche from an excess of spiritual excitement.

Communication with spiritual beings is a sacred art that requires practice, inner silence, and detachment. It is not about accumulating answers or seeking extraordinary phenomena, but about refining the soul so that it can dialogue with the invisible without distortions.

The operator who develops this listening is transformed—they become more sensitive, just, intuitive, and aligned with the truth. With time, they learn that the true miracle lies not only in the answer but in the silent bond that is established with the spiritual world.

The request made with humility and genuine faith is always heard, even if the answer comes in a different way than expected. Sometimes, it manifests as an imperceptible inner change, as a peace that arises without cause, or as a synchronicity that confirms the path. And even when silence persists, it carries within it a wisdom that surpasses words—like the night sky that responds to the gaze with stars.

The true merit of spiritual communication lies in the operator's continuous willingness to empty themself, to listen, and to trust. More than seeking immediate results, the deep commitment is to the personal transformation that the rite provokes—a slow unveiling of the self in the presence of the sacred. When the soul learns to recognize the signs without demanding that they conform to its desires, and when the heart welcomes even silence as a gift, the practice ceases to be a mere ceremonial exercise and becomes a path of initiation. In this state of consciousness, each rite is an invisible step towards the luminous center of existence, where language is made not only with words but with the very vibration of being in communion with the eternal.

Chapter 13
The Ritual Farewell

The closing of a magical ritual is as sacred as its preparation and execution. Conjuring angels and spirits requires not only technique and reverence but also a careful, dignified, and safe conclusion. In the system of the *Heptameron*, the ritual farewell represents the finalization of the established spiritual link. Its purpose is not only to thank and release the summoned entities but also to restore the energetic integrity of the operator and the environment. An incomplete or negligent closing can leave the operator vulnerable, emotionally unstable, or energetically exposed. For this reason, the ritual farewell must be understood as a second apex within the magical practice—a moment of extreme lucidity, where what was erected with solemnity is dissolved with respect.

Over the centuries, magicians from different traditions have noticed that the energetic residues of a poorly closed ritual not only disturb the operator's auric field but can also permeate the physical environment with a sense of restlessness or subtle oppression. These invisible traces behave like unresolved echoes, attracting the attention of wandering entities or causing interference in subsequent rituals. In more severe cases, episodes of recurrent insomnia, mood swings, the breaking of consecrated objects, or even disturbances in the behavior of household animals have been recorded—all symptoms that the spiritual channel remains open beyond the permitted time.

The farewell, therefore, is not just a spiritual formality: it constitutes a practice of energetic and psychic hygiene. Just as a surgeon does not leave the operating room without completing the procedures of asepsis, the magician must not end a spiritual contact without cleansing, sealing, and harmonizing the space. This includes both the external space (circle, altar, instruments) and the internal space of the operator themself—their body, mind, and emotions.

Another often-overlooked aspect is spiritual reciprocity. Luminous entities, especially those linked to the celestial spheres, respond with more fullness and willingness when they feel that the operator cultivates not only reverence in the call but also honor in the farewell. The absence of an appropriate closing can compromise future conjurations, generate truncated responses, or even completely silence the manifestation of the higher intelligences. After all, no relationship, not even with the invisible, flourishes where recognition and courtesy are lacking.

It is also relevant to mention that the ritual farewell operates as a vibrational reconfiguration. By ending the rite, the operator transitions from an altered state of consciousness—where their field expands, their sensitivity sharpens, and the veils between worlds become thin—to a state of integration and recollection.

This transition should not be abrupt. It requires precise gestures, significant words, and sufficient time for the soul to re-accompany the body, returning to daily life without scattered fragments or still-ajar portals.

In the *Heptameron*, each step of the farewell is constructed as a descending step on the mystical ladder. By giving thanks, the operator acknowledges the gift received; by formally closing, they re-establish the boundaries between worlds; by sprinkling and sealing the circle, they deactivate the ritual mechanisms with delicacy; by silencing and disrobing, they resume their ordinary identity with respect and presence. None of these gestures is superfluous—all are part of a subtle engineering aimed at protecting, nurturing, and balancing the spiritual being who dared to touch the eternal.

Therefore, the farewell is not just the end of a rite. It is the final consecration of the lived experience. A space where the invisible departs with dignity, and the visible reorganizes itself with beauty. Where the magician, having received, gives back; having opened, closes; having ascended, returns—not as one who goes back to the starting point, but as one who descends from the mountain with their face still bathed in light.

- The Moment of the Farewell

Upon perceiving that the communication with the spirit has come to an end—whether through a received response, prolonged silence, or an internal indication of termination—the operator must begin the process of farewell. The initiative should never be abrupt. On the contrary, the departure should be measured, respectful, and liturgically significant.

"All that is opened with reverence must be closed with greater reverence."

This principle is not just an ethical guideline but a vibrational anchor that protects the operator when transiting between planes. The end of communication requires sensitivity to perceive the natural exhaustion of the spiritual flow. Often, the spirit subtly withdraws before the operator rationally realizes it. It is up to the practitioner to develop an inner listening to recognize this instant: a shiver that ceases, an atmosphere that dissolves, a sudden sensation of returning to the density of time.

Upon identifying this threshold, the operator must act with contemplative precision. The first gesture is internal: to breathe deeply, three times, in a conscious manner, allowing the body to begin reconnecting with the gravity of ordinary reality. Next, aligning the spine is more than a physical posture—it is a symbolic gesture of resuming one's own axis, of affirming the sovereignty of the incarnate self after the immersion in the higher spheres.

The gaze, until then perhaps turned inward, towards the center of the circle, or to the focus of manifestation, should be slowly redirected to the physical space. This does not mean a loss of sacredness, but a gradual transition of focus, like one walking out of a temple with still-bare feet and a silent heart. Attention must return to the surroundings, to the light of the candles, to the form of the objects, to the ambient sound—all that witnessed the magical operation.

At this moment, the operator must remember the four pillars of the farewell: to thank, to close, to seal, and to disperse. These four verbs are not just external stages, but internal states that the magician must embody with full intention. Thanking acknowledges the gift; closing re-establishes the boundaries; sealing protects the space and the created bond; and dispersing harmonizes the frequencies that remained suspended in the environment.

It is advisable, even before the formal thanksgiving, to take a brief contemplative pause. The operator can place a hand over their heart or over the center of their abdomen and be silent for a few seconds, in silent reverence. This pause acts as an invisible threshold between the time of the spirit and the time of the body—and it favors a more conscious and integrated farewell.

No ritual farewell should be rushed, no matter how brief the contact may have been. Even subtle encounters require a sacred dissolution. And the more potent the spiritual manifestation, the more delicate the disengagement must be. Experienced magicians report that, when they neglect this stage, they feel as if a part of them has been "stuck" in the rite, causing depletion, lethargy, or disturbing dreams in the following days.

Thus, the moment of the farewell is, in fact, the beginning of a new cycle within the same practice. It is when the invisible withdraws with dignity, and the visible must relearn how to contain the sacred without overflowing. All that was evoked with seriousness must be returned with even greater respect. It is in this spirit that the magician's soul remains whole, and the magic circle fulfills its final function: to become once again just space, but now imbued with silence and light.

1. The Thanksgiving

The first step is to express gratitude for the spiritual presence. This is not a mere formality but a vibrational action that acknowledges the summoned intelligence as an essential part of the operation. Gratitude aligns the magician's heart with the celestial order and dissipates any remnant of tension or demand that may have arisen during the rite. This simple gesture, when made with inner truth, seals the bond with dignity and honors the spirit in its sacred nature.

The operator can use formal or spontaneous words, as long as they are sincere and humble. The choice of tone should reflect the elevation of the rite and the character of the evoked entity—the higher its hierarchy, the more reverent the farewell should be. The language can vary according to the practitioner's style but should never slip into a casual or impatient tone. The ideal is for the thanksgiving to be pronounced in a clear voice, with presence and devotion, preferably while looking at the center of the circle or at the place where the spiritual presence was most strongly felt.

Examples of a thanksgiving formula:

"In the name of the Most High, I thank you for your presence and light. May you return in peace to your celestial spheres, and may your virtue remain as a blessing."

"Be praised, O spirit of light, for your manifestation in this sacred circle. In the name of the Creator, your mission is fulfilled."

These formulas, though brief, contain the three essential elements of an effective farewell: the recognition of the divine, the peaceful release of the entity, and a reciprocal blessing. It is important to emphasize that it is not necessary to invent elaborate phrases—what drives the effectiveness of the word is the intention behind it.

Avoid phrases like "you can go now" or "we're done," as they denote a lack of reverence. They break the symbolic field built with effort and can be interpreted as disrespect. Just as an audience with a noble requires protocol upon entry and exit, dealing with spiritual intelligences requires a coherent liturgy from beginning to end.

2. The Formal Closing

After the thanksgiving, the operator must conduct the formal closing of the rite. This is not just a symbolic act: it is a vibrational reintegration of the space to its original state. The practice consists of reciting a traditional prayer or psalm that invokes protection, dissolution of the bond, and elevation of the atmosphere.

In the system of the *Heptameron*, the most commonly used psalms are Psalm 91 ("He who dwells in the shelter of the Most High...")—associated with protection against adverse forces—and Psalm 23 ("The Lord is my shepherd...")—which evokes divine care and safe conduct. These psalms should be recited in a measured voice, allowing each word to reverberate in the space and in the operator's body.

Next, the operator recites the Divine Names traced in the circle: Elohim, El Shaddai, Adonai, Agla.

These names are not chosen at random. Each has its own frequency and represents distinct attributes of the divinity:
- Elohim invokes the creative and ordering aspect of the primordial light;
- El Shaddai evokes the presence of protection and fullness;
- Adonai acknowledges the divine sovereignty over all manifest forms;
- Agla (an acrostic for "*Atha Gibor Leolam Adonai*") powerfully seals the continuity of the divine presence in time.

The recitation of these names re-establishes the spiritual order and dissolves the bridge between the worlds. It acts as a vibrational clasp that closes the access way opened at the beginning of the operation. After pronouncing the names, the operator can make the sign of the cross, slightly bow their head, or extend their hands in a gesture of closing, according to their personal tradition.

This step, when performed with lucidity and fervor, has the power to stabilize the field, ward off any remaining influence, and prepare the space for the subsequent stages of the farewell. It is the moment when sacred time begins to give way again to common time—not with haste, but with solemnity.

3. The Aspersion of Holy Water

The circle is then sprinkled with holy water or lustral water. This gesture, though simple at first glance, carries a profound symbolic and vibrational power. The consecrated water acts not only as a vehicle of purification but as an element of reconnection between the divine and the terrestrial. When cast upon the ground of the circle, it dissolves possible residual tensions, seals open passages, and reintegrates the space into its natural conditions.

The operator should walk slowly in a counter-clockwise direction—a movement that symbolizes the reversal of the opening process—and, with a sprig of hyssop, rosemary, or even with their own fingers, carefully sprinkle the water along the circumference of the circle. Each step should be conscious, rhythmic, as if each drop were landing to appease and cleanse the veils between worlds.

During this gesture, one recites again:

"Asperges me, Domine, hyssopo, et mundabor: lavabis me, et super nivem dealbabor."

This prayer from Psalm 51 (Psalm 50 in some traditions)—traditional in Christian liturgy—means: "Purify me with hyssop, and I shall be clean; wash me, and I shall be whiter than snow." The pronunciation of these words should be done in a solemn tone, allowing the sound, intention, and gesture to intertwine in a single ritual flow. The aspersion need not be abundant, but it must be precise and complete, covering the entire edge of the circle and, if possible, also the center, where the spiritual manifestation was most intense.

This moment marks the definitive deactivation of the opened spiritual channels, functioning as a kind of aquatic and sacred "closing key." In many traditions, it is believed that water has memory and can transmute subtle fields—which is why its presence at the end of an evocation is indispensable.

4. The Closing of the Circle

The most important part of the farewell is the symbolic closing of the magic circle. This stage represents the final seal of the operation and the complete return to ordinary reality. The operator must, with a wand or ritual sword, erase the visible traces drawn on the ground—if chalk, charcoal, or another graphic element was used—with firm and continuous movements, always in a counter-clockwise direction.

If the circle was traced with ephemeral elements, such as sand or flour, these should be gently dispersed. If it is set up on a consecrated cloth or ritual rug, the operator should fold or roll it up with attention and a clear intention of closing. This gesture should be accompanied by a ritual phrase, which can be said in a firm voice, while the gaze remains attentive to the limits of the space:

"May this circle now be closed to the eyes of men and of spirits. May all passage dissolve under the light of the One."

This proclamation is more than a statement: it acts as an energetic command, dissolving any remaining link and sealing the environment. The magician should visualize, while performing this act, a luminous contraction of the space—as if the magical field were being gently absorbed back into the Source.

It is fundamental that the closing of the circle be done with clarity of intention. It should never be left half-done, at the risk of leaving the space vulnerable. When well-executed, this gesture transmits to the body and soul the security that the journey has been completed and that the sacred, duly honored, has been withdrawn in peace.

5. The Final Incense

A final, light incense should be burned, as a sign of gratitude and as a disperser of the concentrated energies. The smoke, an ancestral symbol of the spirit in ascent, functions in this context as a vehicle of harmonization. It is no longer about evoking or purifying, but about pacifying, equalizing the fields, and allowing the frequencies to settle gently.

The use of resins and herbs of a gentle and welcoming nature is suggested: sandalwood, lavender, light frankincense, or benzoin. The operator should walk with the censer around the magical space, making the circuit in a clockwise direction this time, symbolizing the reintegration of the space into the profane world. While fanning the smoke in the four cardinal directions, the magician can say in a soft and conscious voice:

"Go in peace, spirit of light. May this smoke carry with it the blessing you have left."

These words seal the sharing between planes and help to re-establish the vibrational balance of the environment. The smoke should be observed with attention: its density, direction, or unusual behavior may offer clues about the still-active presence of some force. If this occurs, the operator can prolong the fumigation until they feel the field is lighter and quieter.

The final incense not only concludes the rite—it consecrates the return to the ordinary with beauty, gentleness, and reverence. After its use, the environment remains imbued with a discreet and sacred perfume, like a final breeze that bears witness to the presence of the invisible and its departure in peace.

6. Reverence and Silence

With the formal rites concluded, the operator should sit inside the empty circle or next to it and maintain a moment of deep silence. This pause is more than a formality: it is an immersion into inner listening, a suspension of ordinary time where the soul has a chance to reorganize itself after contact with the sacred.

During this time:
- Feel the body again;
- Breathe deeply for a few minutes;
- Let the mind rest without images or questions.

The ideal is for this quietude to last between seven and fifteen minutes, but its value is not in the duration, but in the quality of the surrender. It is a liminal space, where the operator does not speak, does not write, does not move excessively—they simply remain. The stillness allows the more subtle layers of the being to restructure, helping to integrate spiritual perceptions that might otherwise dissipate or cause emotional disharmony.

This moment of recollection allows consciousness to return to the everyday plane with serenity. It is also when one perceives the energetic integration of what was experienced. Sometimes, during this silence, small understandings emerge: a word heard during the rite gains new meaning; an image fixes itself with archetypal clarity; an emotion quiets down and reveals its true origin.

The ritual silence, in this context, is not empty: it is a matrix. It is the womb of magical assimilation, the place where the invisible lodges and begins to become part of the real.

7. Disrobing with Intention

The ritual garments should be removed with care and folded with gratitude. This act should not be done as a mechanical gesture, but as an essential part of the farewell. The clothing worn during the rite acts as a symbolic second skin—it carries in its fibers the energy of what was experienced. Therefore, upon taking it off, the operator must maintain the awareness that they are also divesting themself of the expanded state of consciousness.

While doing so, the operator can say:

"Just as I wore the sacred, I now disrobe in peace. May the invisible mantle of light remain upon me."

This formula helps to maintain the spiritual connection, even after the closing of the rites. Folding the garments, instead of dropping them, is an act of respect—for the rite, for the body, and for the invisible. Some practitioners prefer to wrap them in a white or dark blue cloth and store them separately from common clothes. This reinforces the sacred character of the attire and prevents its vibration from mixing with the everyday.

This act symbolically closes the altered state of consciousness and returns the magician to their ordinary condition, without losing the spiritual connection.

8. Post-Ritual Hygiene

It is suggested that the operator wash their hands, face, and, if possible, take a brief bath with warm water and gentle herbs like lavender, basil, or rosemary. More than a physical cleaning, this bath functions as a kind of dissolution of the ritual aura. The warm water helps to discharge accumulated static electricity and to bring the body back to a state of energetic rest.

The herbs, in turn, act as bridges between the planes—each with its own vibrational signature. Lavender calms and pacifies the emotional field; basil strengthens psychic integrity; rosemary invigorates and cleanses subtle impurities.

Avoid:
- Immediately turning on electronic devices;
- Talking to many people right after the ritual;
- Eating in excess or engaging in agitated activities.

These actions, common in modern daily life, abruptly break the field of expanded sensitivity and can cause a sensation of "vibrational shock." The ideal is to maintain recollection for at least an hour after the ceremony. This silent time helps to consolidate the effects of the rite, allowing the magic to settle into the deeper layers of the psyche.

This set of cares closes the rite not only on the spiritual plane but also on the physical one. It is like closing a book with respect, knowing that the last page is as important as the first. And in this clean and intentional silence, what was received begins, at last, to flourish within.

9. Final Thanksgiving to the Divine

Before completely leaving the magical space, the operator should kneel (if possible) and recite a prayer of gratitude to the Creator. This is the most intimate moment of the farewell—there are no more evoked spirits, no external presence to be honored. All that remains is the sacred bond between the magician and the One. Kneeling, when physically possible, is a gesture that confesses humility and acknowledges that every magical operation is, deep down, a gift granted and not an individual achievement.

"Most High, source of life and truth, I thank you for allowing this sacred contact. May what has been done be established in goodness, and may your light accompany me on the visible and invisible paths."

This prayer seals the experience as part of the operator's spiritual destiny, anchoring the practice not just in technique, but in devotion. One can also use other spontaneous words, as long as they are born from a sincere heart. This final thanksgiving transcends the rite performed: it is a renewal of the pact between the practitioner and the Mystery, between the soul and its origin.

The ideal is for this thanksgiving to be done with a lowered forehead, closed eyes, and rested hands—or in an offering mudra, if one so desires. The important thing is that the gesture, the word, and the intention are united in the same frequency of reverence. In that instant, the magician ceases to be an officiant and becomes once again a disciple of the light, a walker of the invisible who knows how to be grateful even for what was not fully understood.

10. Signs of a Good Closing

After a well-conducted closing, the operator typically perceives:
- A sensation of peace and serenity;
- Mental clarity;
- An energized but calm body;
- An absence of fear or obsession with the ritual;
- Elevated intuition in the following hours.

These signs are not guarantees, but indications. They point to the fact that the spiritual field was closed cleanly and that the invoked energy was well assimilated. They also indicate that the operator has returned to their center without ruptures or dispersions.

If you feel fatigue, disorientation, or agitation, it is recommended to:
- Sleep well that night;
- Use an anchoring crystal (like hematite or onyx);
- Repeat a short prayer as an anchor.

These simple practices help to rebalance the energy field and to sediment the effects of the rite. It is important to remember that, even with all the correct procedures, the soul may need more time to assimilate what was experienced—especially if the operation touched deep aspects of the unconscious or if there was a very intense manifestation.

The ritual farewell is, in fact, the beginning of the assimilation of all that was received. It is the moment when magic descends from the heavens and begins to take root in the everyday. The operator who closes with reverence not only protects themselves but also honors the bond created with the subtle realms. They leave the circle as one who returns from an invisible sanctuary—not with haste, but with gratitude. Not with pride, but with presence.

Never dismiss the importance of this stage. Magic is a spiral—it begins in the visible world, ascends to the higher planes, but must descend again, with grace and order, to the terrestrial plane. Only in this way can what was touched on high flourish on earth. And it is in the art of the farewell that this descent is realized, not as a fall, but as a blessing.

To close a rite is to seal a silent pact between the visible and the invisible, allowing the operator's soul to rest within itself again with fullness. When each gesture of the farewell is made with presence and intention, the vibrational field realigns, and the transcendent experience finds a dwelling in the body and in memory. It is not just about closing a cycle, but about dignifying the sacred with the same nobility with which it was invoked. The magician who bids farewell with reverence does not just close a magic circle—they consecrate, within themselves, the continuity of a path where every rite lived becomes a living part of their spiritual journey.

Chapter 14
Records and Post-Ritual Care

The post-ritual stage, frequently neglected by neophytes, is fundamental for consolidating the effects of the magical operation, integrating the teachings received, and ensuring the operator's spiritual stability. The *Heptameron* does not end with the farewell to the spirit: it extends into the silence that comes after, in the notes made with reverence, in the attitudes of daily life that reveal spiritual maturity. It is in this invisible space between the magical gesture and common life that the true alchemy operates—a discreet but profound transmutation of the self. The operator who abandons the circle without preparing the ground for what comes next runs the risk of transforming a sacred experience into an empty act, with scattered or even harmful effects.

Often, the post-ritual phase is where the soul, still sensitive and open, becomes vulnerable to both external interferences and the internal traps of the ego. It is when the chants cease and the candles are extinguished that the true voices begin to speak—and not all of them are luminous. Therefore, just as important as knowing the names of the angels or the planetary hours is cultivating the serene and vigilant listening that can only flourish in the conscious quietude of the following days. This listening is not learned in grimoires but in the attentive repetition of practice, in diligent writing, and in the loving observation of oneself.

This chapter provides detailed guidance on how to create a magical diary, record experiences with discernment, and protect oneself energetically after the ritual. It also offers advice on how to deal with secondary effects, interpret received symbols, and maintain emotional integrity along the initiatory path. It is a manual for internal support, an anchor for the soul that has just navigated deep waters and now needs to reach the shore safely. Because it is not enough to evoke: one must welcome, understand, and transform what has been received. Every image, every sensation, every silence laden with meaning must be honored as a fragment of the Mystery.

By establishing a commitment to continuous recording, the operator learns to recognize the subtle cycles of magical practice—moments of expansion, recollection, revelation, and purification. A well-maintained ritual diary becomes a faithful mirror of the hidden journey, revealing not only successes and failures but, above all, patterns of spiritual learning that repeat, evolve, and sometimes require revisiting. This sacred notebook is not a luxury but a necessity, especially when dealing with intelligences that operate on planes where language is symbolic and time is spiral.

Furthermore, the post-ritual phase is the time for conscious choices. The way one returns to the world after contact with the invisible says much about the degree of integration achieved. Small actions—such as caring for a plant, cleaning the altar with reverence, or offering silence instead of hasty words—are gestures of ritual continuity. They say to the spiritual world: "I heard. I respect. I am willing to live what I have received." The post-ritual period is not an interval between ceremonies but an active part of the invisible liturgy that sustains the bridge between worlds.

Finally, it is in the careful living of this suspended time that the operator begins to develop true spiritual authority. Not the kind that comes from technical mastery of formulas or the frequency of practices, but the kind that springs from a deep rooting in the real, from the ability to remain centered in the face of mystery. A silent, serene, non-negotiable authority—one that does not need to assert itself because it manifests naturally in every gesture, every choice, every unspoken word. The philosopher's stone of magic lies not only in the successful conjuration but in the transformed life that results from it.

- 1. The Magical Diary: A Journey's Companion

Every serious operator should keep a ritualistic diary. This notebook is not a simple repository of memories but a tool for self-knowledge, discernment, and spiritual evolution. To write down each magical experience is like drawing a map of one's own soul on its journey through the veils of the invisible. Over time, this record transforms into a silent testimony of the initiatory path, revealing not only what was experienced on the ritualistic plane but also how one reacted, learned, and was transformed by it.

The act of writing after a rite has an alchemical power. It forces the operator to revisit the experience with calmness, filtering the emotion of the moment and allowing the awakened consciousness to dialogue with the deeper layers of the self. In doing so, a second stage of the magical work begins: spiritual digestion. It is in this process that many intuitions are revealed, that symbolic messages settle into understanding, and that the subtle echoes of the evocation find form and meaning.

- What to record:
    - Date, time, and location of the ritual;
    - Day of the week and magical season;
    - Objective of the conjuration;
    - Physical, emotional, and mental state before the start;
    - Words used and any improvisations;
    - Sensations during the ritual: visions, sounds, emotions;
    - Responses or perceptions received;
    - Technical difficulties or distractions;
    - State after the ritual: physical, mental, spiritual.

This information will help the operator to identify patterns, evolutions, and recurring challenges. Over time, it will be possible to perceive how certain hours favor deeper results, how the emotional state can influence the clarity of spiritual communication, or how certain psalms or seals resonate more with the individual nature of the one who uses them. The diary thus becomes a silent ally in the art of refining the inner instrument that we are.

- Recommended form: Use a notebook consecrated solely for this purpose. The consecration can be done with a brief prayer of intention and the use of a gentle incense, passing the notebook through the smoke with reverence. It is recommended that the cover bear a personal symbol of protection or consecration, be it a sigil created by the operator or a psalm written by hand. It can also contain seals of the evoked spirits, drawings of the circles used, biblical verses, or psalms that have particularly touched the heart.

Some operators prefer to separate the diary into sections: before, during, and after the ritual. Others write freely, mixing narrative with reflections, prayers, and even dreams that occurred in the following days—anything that, in some way, is connected to the ritual experience. The important thing is the continuity and honesty with which one writes. It is not about producing a technical report for others, but an intimate testimony before the sacred.

Over time, rereading previous entries can become a powerful practice. In the light of accumulated experience, old enigmas become clear, and repetitive mistakes become visible. Sometimes, what was not understood at first is revealed with clarity months or years later, as the operator matures. The diary, therefore, is not just a mirror of the moment but a compendium of spiritual evolution that grows and breathes with the magician themself.

- 2. How to Evaluate the Experience

After the ritual, enthusiasm can lead to exaggerated interpretations. It is important to maintain objectivity, even in the face of intense phenomena.

Ask yourself:
- Was what I felt authentic or a mental projection?
- Was there coherence between what I asked for and what I received?
- Did the spirit respond, or was it my expectation?
- Did the energy of the environment change visibly?
- Was there a lasting spiritual resonance in the following days?

The maturity of the magician is revealed in the ability to separate fantasy from real experience, without losing the enchantment of the sacred.

- 3. Interpretation of Symbols and Responses

Often, spirits communicate through mental images, symbols, single words, thermal or luminous sensations. The diary helps to map these elements over time.

- Examples:
    - A white rose can represent peace, reconciliation, or the purity of the request.
    - A sword can suggest action, defense, the cutting of illusions, or authority.
    - A ladder can signify spiritual progress or future steps.

There is no universal dictionary. Each symbol must be interpreted in light of the ritual's intention and the operator's personal archetype.

- 4. Post-Ritual Energetic Care

After an evocation, the operator's energy field remains more open for a few hours or even days. This requires sensitive and continuous vigilance, as any dense or dissonant stimulus can interfere with the assimilation of the invoked forces. The post-ritual phase is a liminal state—neither fully inside the circle nor completely outside of it—and, for that very reason, one of extreme delicacy.

In this period, the boundaries between the physical, emotional, and spiritual bodies are more fluid. It is common for the operator to perceive mood swings, an altered perception of time, vivid dreams, or even a sensation of "leaking light." Such symptoms are not cause for alarm but are indicative that the soul is still accommodating the energies that were moved. Protection at this time should not be reactive but ritualistic and compassionate, as if the body itself were a temple to be purified and sealed again.

- Avoid arguments, chaotic environments, or excessive consumption of information;
- Avoid different spiritual practices immediately after the ritual (such as oracles or mediumship);
- Avoid repeating the same ritual in sequence without discernment.

In addition to these precautions, it is essential to cultivate spaces of rest and simplicity. It is not necessary to isolate oneself completely, but reducing stimuli—especially digital ones—can help to stabilize the psychosphere. Contact with nature, contemplative art, or even silence can act as spiritual balms in this process.

- Suggestions:
    - Use protective crystals (black tourmaline, onyx, obsidian);
    - Take light baths with calming herbs (chamomile, lavender);
    - Use candles or incense moderately in the following days;
    - Physical grounding through walking in nature or gardening.

These elements do not replace consciousness, but support it. A bath with lavender leaves can be prepared as follows: boil a handful of the herbs in clean water, let it cool to a warm temperature, and pour it over the body after a hygienic bath, always from the neck down, while visualizing the release of spiritual residues and the return to the inner axis. Walking barefoot on the earth, watering plants with attention, or even preparing a meal with presence are ways to "ground" the spirit, to bring the soul back into the body with gentleness and reverence.

- 5. Avoid the Rebound Effect

The magical ego can inflate after an intense experience. Feeling "chosen" or "special" is a classic symptom of spiritual imbalance. There is a legitimate fascination in contact with higher intelligences, but also a danger: the illusion of superiority. The true operator recognizes that any manifestation obtained is a grace, not a personal achievement. The spirit communicates because there is an opening and permission from the Most High, not because of the evoker's isolated merit.

To avoid this:
- Maintain humility: everything comes from the Most High, not from you;
- Share sparingly: do not trivialize your experience with disbelievers or the curious;
- Pray for discernment before speaking about what you saw or heard;
- Do not try to repeat the experience compulsively. Magic is not a spectacle.

It is recommended that, at the end of the rite, the operator offers a silent prayer of thanks and symbolically offers the fruits of the practice to the greater good. This inner gesture—even without words—helps to redirect the focus to spiritual service, diluting the risk of idolizing one's own experience.

- 6. Integration with Daily Life

True magic is that which transforms living. After a ritual:
- Observe changes in your mood, dreams, and relationships in the following days;
- Pay attention to synchronicities (repeated words, encounters, intersecting readings);
- Take small actions that symbolize your openness to the received message: donate something, write a letter, start a new habit.

Integration is the cornerstone of the post-ritual phase. Without it, the ritual remains an isolated event with no real consequence. With it, every daily gesture becomes an unfolding of the sacred, a continuation of the magic circle in the fabric of common life. The operator who learns to live the echoes of the ritual in the details of the day—in the way they listen to someone, arrange their home, or act in the face of a challenge—becomes, in fact, an alchemist of the invisible. The evocation, then, ceases to be an end in itself and becomes a bridge: between planes, between realities, between who we were and who we can become.

- 7. When to Repeat the Ritual?

It is not always necessary to repeat a rite. The ego's impatience can press for immediate results, but the language of the spiritual world does not obey human time. There are times when silence is, in itself, an answer. To insist on a new call without fully listening to the echo of the previous one is like knocking again on a door that is still opening.

Before considering a repetition, ask yourself if there was, in fact, an absence of a response, or if your perception has not yet matured enough to recognize it. Many signs are revealed in the subsequent days, in dreams, synchronicities, or intuitive flashes that escape the logical mind. Haste, on the other hand, tends to generate noise and to close the subtle channels that were opened with the rite.

Do it again only if:
- The response was ambiguous and you feel there was noise in the connection;
- The conjuration was interrupted by external factors (noises, distractions, failures);
- There was a serious error in the execution: an incomplete circle, the wrong date, impure materials.

When repetition is necessary, prepare with even more care than the first time. Review the previous diary entry, study the possible errors with humility, and reconsecrate your instruments. Avoid using magic as an escape valve. Obsessive repetition wears out the spiritual field and can attract illusory thought-forms—simulacra of the original experience, devoid of truth and laden with unconscious desire.

- 8. Failures and Frustrations: How to Deal with Them

If the ritual seems to have "failed," avoid harsh self-criticism. Magic is a living art, subject to multiple variables. An evocation does not always produce immediate or perceptible effects. Often, what was planted in that moment will only flourish weeks or months later, when the internal ground is more fertile.

The causes of failure are diverse, and all offer an invitation to self-knowledge:

- Lack of emotional preparation;
- Confused or selfish intention;
- Misalignment with the spiritual principles of the rite;
- Presence of unconscious fears that block the connection.

In these cases, record everything with honesty. Name your fears, doubts, hesitations. Sometimes, writing down one's own frustration is already a rite of release and healing. Reflect, pray, and wait at least one lunar cycle (28 days) before trying again. Time, in magic, is a hidden ally—it allows the waters to clarify and the intention to mature in depth.

- 9. Protection Against Side Effects

Although rare, some side effects may arise. They do not necessarily indicate an error, but rather a heightened sensitivity or an ongoing energetic reorganization:
- Symbolic nightmares;
- Irritability without cause;
- Disrupted sleep or insomnia;
- Disproportionate apathy or euphoria.

The body and psyche respond to the spiritual opening in different ways. Sometimes, an excess of light reveals shadows that were dormant. The important thing is to welcome these signs without fear or judgment, and to act with gentleness and firmness.

Recommended actions:
- Purify the bedroom with gentle incense and coarse salt in bowls;
- Place an amethyst or quartz stone under the pillow;
- Say a brief and sincere nightly prayer before sleeping;
- Eat well and avoid prolonged fasting after the ritual.

If the symptoms persist for more than seven days, seek spiritual guidance from someone experienced, who can help discern between a natural unfolding and an imbalance that needs to be treated with more attention.

- 10. Silence as a Continuation of the Ritual

After the ceremony ends, maintain a fast from words for a few hours—or even days—about what occurred. This silence is not fear; it is maturity. It is in silence that the echoes of the experience deepen, like seeds that only germinate in the darkness of the earth. Talking too much dissipates the force, confuses the memory, and weakens the soul.

"Silence is the guardian of magical truth."

Only share your experience with:
- Trusted mentors;
- Fellow practitioners who know the system;
- Mirrors of the soul—people whose sacred presence can welcome without judging.

The word, when finally spoken, should come from a place of settlement and not of exhibition. To record, to care, to interpret, and to integrate are sacred verbs in the post-ritual phase. And silence, more than the absence of sound, is the frame where the soul draws, little by little, the meaning of what it has lived.

To record, to care, to interpret, and to integrate are sacred verbs in the post-ritual phase. The operator who dedicates attention to this stage of the process shows not only devotion but a commitment to their own inner transformation. It is in these gestures that the rite continues to live, no longer in the circle traced on the ground, but in the invisible spiral that is drawn in the soul. Each note made with sincerity, each silence chosen with consciousness, each daily action laden with symbolism reveals that the magic did not end with the spirit's farewell—it has only changed its form.

True power resides not in the instant of the conjuration, but in the ability to sustain the vibration of the sacred in ordinary time. It is easy to don the ritual mantle and intone ancient words; it is difficult to allow the evocation to resonate in every subsequent choice, in every cultivated thought, in every bond maintained or transformed. The post-ritual phase is this testing ground: there it is revealed whether the magic was a performative act or an internal commitment to the Mystery.

The *Heptameron* is not a grimoire of spectacle but an initiatory map. Each conjuration is a step on the ladder of the soul. And it is in the silences between the rites that the rough stone begins to reveal its polished facets. Not by the momentary brilliance of the vision, but by the persistence with which the operator returns to the invisible altar of daily life, where everything is a rite—if there is presence. The ladder is not made only of invocations, but of pauses, doubts, reflections, and rebirths. To ascend is to remain: present, lucid, and faithful to the call that, once heard, is never entirely silenced.

It is on this silent journey, between attentive records and daily gestures laden with meaning, that the true legacy of the practice is revealed. More than an isolated moment of connection with the invisible, the rite unfolds into a pedagogy of presence, where every step outside the circle still echoes the initial call. By honoring the post-ritual phase with the same reverence dedicated to the conjuration, the operator transforms their very life into fertile ground for the sacred, allowing magic to infiltrate the fibers of common existence until, little by little, there is no longer a boundary between the ritual and life itself.

Chapter 15
Ethics and Dangers of the Art

Upon reaching the final steps of this ritualistic ladder, it is imperative that the practitioner pauses to reflect deeply on the ethics that sustain the entire edifice of ceremonial magic. The *Heptameron*, although a practical work, is founded on spiritual values that cannot be neglected. Magic without ethics is manipulation. Ritual without humility is vanity. And evocation without discernment can become an open portal to imbalance and illusion.

Before proceeding, it is necessary to recognize that true spiritual power does not manifest solely through symbols, formulas, and ritual procedures. It requires, above all, an inner integration that supports every gesture with moral clarity and sensitivity. Many scholars get lost in seeking only tangible results from ceremonial work, forgetting that the magical operation is, in essence, a communion with the invisible—and the invisible only reveals itself legitimately to a pure heart.

This is not about spiritual puritanism, but about a mature understanding of the pact that magic demands. Every traced circle, every intoned divine name, every lit incense is a declaration: "I am ready to act as a bridge between worlds, and I assume the responsibility for it."

When this consciousness is absent, the ritual transforms into a theatrical imitation, incapable of producing any real transformation—or worse, it opens breaches for forces that respond to desire, but not to truth.

This is the point where ethics becomes more than an abstract principle: it reveals itself as a safeguard for one's own sanity. The operator who acts without discernment can easily confuse a symbolic manifestation of the unconscious with an objective spiritual presence. The line between revelation and delusion is often thin—and only inner honesty can preserve it.

There is also a constant risk of instrumentalizing the practice. Upon realizing that certain rites produce effects, it is common for the ego to desire control over these effects for personal ends. Then arises the temptation to invoke not what is necessary, but what pleases; to evoke not what guides, but what obeys. This deviation, though subtle at first, tends to grow like a weed, suffocating the spiritual root of the practice.

Therefore, this chapter invites the reader to understand the limits of magical practice, the risks of pride, the difference between invocation and evocation, and the responsibility that accompanies spiritual power. It is not enough to know how to operate the elements: one must know why and for whom one operates. Every magical action reverberates not only in the invisible world but also in the soul of the magician themself. Like the alchemist who sees in the crucible the reflection of their psyche, the ritual operator needs to understand that every evocation is, in part, a dialogue with their own shadows.

It is, ultimately, a call to maturity. Magic is not a path for those seeking escape, glory, or distraction, but for those who have the courage to transform themselves. And transformation, on this path, means letting go of the illusions of control and accepting mystery as a master. Ethics, in this context, is not an external code, but an internal vibration that guides every choice, every silence, and every word pronounced before the altar.

- 1. Invocation vs. Evocation: Internal and External Doors

A classic distinction in the magical tradition is between invoking and evoking. Although both terms involve calling upon spiritual forces, their natures are distinct:

- To invoke means to call inward—to draw the presence of a spiritual force into one's own being. This is what occurs, for example, in states of deep prayer, when one asks for the presence of an angel, an archetype, or a virtue. In these moments, the operator becomes a receptacle and a mirror, allowing the invoked energy to penetrate their consciousness and shape their thoughts, attitudes, and inner dispositions. This presence, when legitimate, does not impose itself as a strange voice, but as an increase in lucidity, compassion, or courage. It is a subtle dialogue between the Self and the Transpersonal. However, this fusion can generate imbalances if the practitioner lacks emotional grounding: a mistaken identification with the entity or a hypertrophy of the ego disguised as enlightenment can occur.

- To evoke, on the other hand, is to call forth—to cause a spiritual entity to manifest in a separate space, usually delimited by a magic circle. The spirit, in this case, does not enter the magician but appears in their presence, as if responding to a ceremonial call in a sacred audience chamber. This operation requires ritual discipline, symbolic mastery, and psychic firmness. Unlike invocation, which demands inner openness, evocation requires precise delimitation: the circle is the boundary between worlds, and the triangle, the place of the entity's manifestation. Evocation is an encounter between distinct consciousnesses, where the operator must maintain clarity, composure, and ethical command.

Evocation is more demanding, as it requires containment, purification, and authority. Containment prevents fear or arrogance from interfering with the rite. Purification ensures that the operator does not bring emotional residues with them that could distort communication. And authority—spiritual, not theatrical—sets the tone of the encounter. Without these qualities, the magician runs the risk of being deceived by projections of their own unconscious or of opening doors to deceitful forces. The magician who does not understand this difference may confuse an expansion of consciousness with delusion, or a symbolic manifestation with an objective presence. It requires maturity to recognize one's own limits and humility to accept that not all that glitters comes from the light.

- 2. The Danger of Magical Pride

Few poisons are as subtle and fatal as pride on the magical path. It manifests as follows:
- A feeling of spiritual superiority over others;
- A desire to impress with magical stories;
- A search for spectacular results as proof of power;
- A belief that one is above natural or spiritual laws.

This type of pride does not appear abruptly—it insinuates itself through small achievements, received compliments, or intense visions that are poorly understood. As the operator begins to perceive the effects of magical practice, they become vulnerable to the temptation of believing that these effects are proof of their personal greatness. Magic, when used as a mirror for the ego, transforms into a stage. The altar becomes a showcase, the rite a performance. And the contact with the sacred, which requires inner silence, gives way to noisy vanity.

Magical pride not only corrupts the intention: it weakens the spiritual field. By inflating themselves, the operator moves away from attunement with higher intelligences, opening space for illusory forms—entities that feed vanity, confirm fantasies, and drain energy. Many initiates stagnate at this point. Instead of proceeding on the path of purification, they remain in delusions of grandeur, convinced they have reached the summit. They do not realize that the further one advances, the more humility is required. True spiritual power is silent, detached, and attentive to the suffering of others—it is never an instrument of self-promotion.

- 3. Spiritual Consent

Evoking a spirit is a sacred act. Even angels, who are messengers of Good, are not available for futile or arbitrary whims. Every evocation needs to be anchored in:

- A just and elevated motive (healing, guidance, protection, revelation);
- An intention clean of manipulation, revenge, or domination;
- A spiritual consent—obtained through inner alignment and the humility of the invoker.

This consent is not a verbal or visible permission but an internal resonance that indicates the operation is in harmony with the spiritual order. Without this attunement, the operator may end up evoking something that responds to their desire—but not to their well-being. An evocation made out of curiosity, whim, or vanity is like knocking on the door of the invisible without knowing who might answer. The spiritual universe does not bow to the human will like a servant. It responds to the truth of the intention.

This is why the masters of the Art have always emphasized inner preparation before the rite: fasting, silence, examination of conscience. The magician needs to verify if their motivation is clean, if their mind is clear, if there is a real need in the call. Otherwise, what responds to the intoned name may not be a legitimate spirit, but a thought-form, an unconscious fragment, or even an opportunistic intelligence. The consequences of this range from the weakening of the energy field to serious psychic imbalances. Evocation, when done with reverence and discernment, becomes a bridge to knowledge. But when done without spiritual consent, it transforms into a trap.

- 4. The Misuse of Magic

There are four common ways to deviate from magical ethics:

1. Manipulating the will of others—even with good intentions, this violates free will. Magic should assist, not control. Forcing someone to make a decision, desire something, or move closer or further away through ritualistic influence is a violation of the invisible pact of spiritual autonomy that sustains all sacred coexistence. It is like trying to impose, by invisible force, a will that is not natural to the other—which generates not only energetic imbalance but also a karmic return in the form of confusion, distance, or guilt.
2. Seeking disproportionate material advantages—it is legitimate to ask for sustenance, work, or protection, but using spirits as servants for selfish gain is dangerous and limiting. The line between need and greed can be thin, and many magicians cross it when they try to instrumentalize the invisible for purposes of power, accumulation, or ostentation. These requests tend to attract forces that charge a high price, imprisoning the operator in cycles of lack and spiritual dependence, even if the initial results seem positive.

3. Conjuring out of mere curiosity or for entertainment—evocation is not a spectacle. Spirits should not be tested or invoked "to see what happens." This attitude violates the sacredness of the rite and attracts disconnected, sometimes chaotic, manifestations that can destabilize the operator's psychic field. To treat the invisible as an amusement park is to make room for forces that mock the sacred and confuse perception. Every evocation is a subtle encounter with the mystery—and the mystery demands reverence.
4. Obsessively repeating rituals to get what one desires—this denotes attachment and a lack of faith. The ritual is a bridge, not a lever. When the magical gesture is repeated with anxiety, it no longer vibrates with the higher order but with the insistence of desire. This creates noise, and the operator ends up moving away from the source, sinking into the illusion that more effort means more power. In truth, the excess of ritual indicates that the magician has stopped trusting—and without trust, the channel closes.
- 5. Psychological and Spiritual Risks

In addition to the spiritual consequences, there are mental risks for those who enter this path without a solid foundation. Some of them are:
- Delusions of grandeur—upon feeling in contact with elevated forces, the operator may begin to believe they are chosen, messianic, or superior to others. This delusion, disguised as enlightenment,

leads to a loss of critical sense and, often, to isolation or the manipulation of other people in the name of a supposed spiritual mission.
- Spiritual paranoia (feeling persecuted by occult forces)—when the magician does not differentiate energetic sensitivity from a real threat, every shadow becomes an enemy. They then live in a constant state of defense, imagining attacks where there is only symbolic movement or an unconscious reflection. This consumes vitality and obscures discernment.
- Social isolation due to a supposed superior spiritual awakening—believing they are misunderstood by the world, the operator withdraws from healthy human bonds. They break with family, with friends, with work, claiming to be "different." Spirituality becomes a refuge for the wounded ego, not a bridge to love.
- Confusion between imagination and spiritual reality—internal visions, dreams, or intuitions are taken as absolute facts. The distinction between what happens in the soul and what happens in the world is lost. This fusion of planes can lead to dissociative states, mystical delusions, or even psychotic episodes.

The protection against this lies in prayer, continuous study, interaction with sensible people, and grounding in everyday reality. Maintaining simple practices, such as caring for the body, handling money responsibly, maintaining dialogue with people who think differently, and frequenting public places, are gestures that help to maintain balance. A spirituality that isolates, that breaks with common life, that creates distortions in affections and in reality, is not elevation—it is escape. True magic flourishes when heaven touches the earth, and the invisible teaches the heart to live with more presence, lucidity, and love.

- 6. The Inner Oath

Before proceeding further with the system of the *Heptameron*, it is recommended that the operator establish an internal pact—not with the spirits, but with their own soul. Something like:

"I swear to seek Knowledge with Reverence, to practice Magic with Truth, to invoke only with a Just Intention, never to manipulate or subjugate anyone, and to honor the Path that has been opened to me."

This commitment is not merely symbolic. It acts as an energetic seal, a silent axis that supports the magician in moments of doubt, temptation, or exaltation. When made with sincerity, the inner oath aligns the operator's purpose with the higher current of the Art, preventing the rite from becoming a tool of the ego. It also serves as a criterion for choice: faced with each magical decision, the operator can ask themself if they are being faithful to that primordial pact.

Furthermore, the oath nurtures the moral field of the practice. Not as a rigid rule imposed from the outside, but as an intimate reminder that ritual power must be exercised with discernment, discretion, and compassion. What is promised to one's own soul echoes on the invisible planes, shaping the quality of the entities that approach, the type of teachings that are revealed, and the direction in which the path opens. A magician without an inner oath is like a ship without a compass: even with strong sails, they can get lost in the sea of their own will.

- 7. The Difference between Authority and Arrogance

Magical authority comes from alignment with the light, from discipline, and from purity of intention. Arrogance is the fruit of haste, comparison, and an inflamed ego. How to distinguish them?

- Authority is silent, firm, and respectful;
- Arrogance is loud, provocative, and insecure.

Legitimate authority does not need to announce itself. It emanates naturally from the magician's presence, manifesting in the clarity of their words, the serenity of their gestures, the coherence of their actions. It is the fruit of a path trodden with humility, effort, and deep listening. Arrogance, on the other hand, seeks to be seen, validated, and feared. It shouts to hide its fragility.

When encountering spiritual resistance, the operator should question their preparation and intention before imposing their command. Not all resistance is malevolent. Sometimes, it is a test—not of the magician's strength, but of the purity of their purpose. Higher spirits do not respond to an authoritarian voice, but to a true vibration. If the operator acts with vanity, haste, or impatience, it is likely they will only attract forces of the same tone—and these hardly lead to the light. True authority is recognized in silence: when the spirit ceases its turmoil and the presence settles with clarity, there has been listening, not imposition.

- 8. The Role of Suffering and Pain

Often, those who come to magic come from a place of pain. Betrayals, losses, illnesses, or oppressions awaken the search for the sacred. This is legitimate—but dangerous if not processed.

Pain can be an opening, but also an abyss. When used as fuel for control, revenge, or self-aggrandizement, it contaminates the rite with the residues of trauma. In this case, the magician does not invoke healing but perpetuates the wound. They use magic as armor, not as a path of liberation.

On the other hand, if suffering is transmuted into compassion, listening, and transformation, it becomes fertile ground for true spiritual power. Pain, when integrated, expands sensitivity, makes the magician more receptive to the mysteries of the invisible, and more conscious of the suffering of others. It purifies motivation, making the magical gesture more silent, more effective, and more generous.

The secret lies in not denying the pain, but in allowing it to teach without dominating. To ritualize suffering is to acknowledge its presence without being enslaved by it. It is to transform the wound into an altar, grief into an offering, and absence into a space for listening. Magic, in this sense, becomes not an escape from pain, but a deep alchemy that redeems it—and, by redeeming it, reveals the true power that springs from honest vulnerability.

- 9. Responsibility Toward Others

Many operators feel the desire to help other people with the rituals of the *Heptameron*. This is possible, provided that:
- There is express permission from the person to be benefited;
- The intention is clear and clean (healing, protection, clarity);
- No energetic or emotional dependency is created with the querent.

Magical practice aimed at another requires even more discernment than practice aimed at oneself. When one acts on behalf of someone else, one also assumes responsibility for that person's field, which implies relevant spiritual and ethical risks. To operate without consent—even with good intentions—is to violate a sacred space that does not belong to us. Magic, in this sense, is not an extension of our will, but a listening to the destiny of the other.

Even more delicate is the risk of establishing bonds of dependency. When assisting someone with rites, there is always the temptation to become necessary, to be seen as an exclusive channel for the sacred. When this occurs, the operator begins to occupy the role of a savior, substituting the querent's own inner path with an external solution. This undermines the spiritual autonomy of the person being helped and distorts the magician's own role.

Remember: to help spiritually is to offer a channel, not a substitute. True assistance happens when the operator empowers the other to walk on their own, to reconnect with their own light, their own inner voice. Therefore, it is fundamental to maintain a focus on simplicity, ethics, and not getting excessively emotionally involved. The operator should remain as a mirror, not as a crutch.

Magical service, when performed with righteousness, can be one of the highest acts on the path. But for this, it needs to be rooted in humility, listening, and a clear awareness that the power is not ours—it only passes through us.

- 10. The Path of Silence and Simplicity

The more elevated the magician, the less need they have to prove anything. The true masters of the Art are discreet, humble, and often unrecognizable. They live their spirituality in the silence of their gestures, in the firmness of their choices, and in an unshakeable ethic.

Magical wisdom is not measured by visions, phenomena, or the number of operations performed. It is recognized in the way the magician walks through the world: without making a fuss, without seeking recognition, without needing to convince anyone of the truth of their experiences. True power is serene.

Therefore:
- Avoid showing off spiritual knowledge on social media;
- Do not try to convert or convince anyone of the effectiveness of your rites;
- Protect your experiences like germinating seeds.

Silence is one of the greatest protections on the path. It guards the mystery, preserves the energy, and prevents vanity or doubt from contaminating the experience. And simplicity is its ally—it shows that what is essential lies not in excesses, but in presence.

Ethics is the anchor of magic. It prevents the operator from getting lost in the waters of illusion, empty power, or inner fragmentation. The *Heptameron*, though ancient, still echoes with a wisdom that demands maturity, reverence, and responsibility.

Magical ethics, far from being a moralistic adornment, is the hidden structure that supports the bridge between worlds. Without it, every rite, no matter how well-executed, becomes as fragile as polished glass: it reflects but breaks easily. The true operator is not the one who evokes the most, but the one who sustains, in every gesture and silence, the vibration of the sacred with integrity. This path requires not only technical mastery but, above all, a living listening of the soul, where the consciousness of the other, humility before the invisible, and fidelity to one's own inner oath intertwine so that magic may be, first and foremost, an expression of truth.

Chapter 16
Visual Appendix and Tables

This final chapter aims to offer the reader visual and practical resources to assist in the precise execution of the rituals presented throughout this work. The practices of the *Heptameron* are highly symbolic and structured, requiring attention to detail and fidelity to the forms. Therefore, we have gathered here diagrams, seals, tables, and translations that will serve as complementary tools for study and ritual action. The appendix should be consulted whenever the operator wishes to confirm essential information, review the layout of the circles, or verify the names, hours, and attributes of the ruling spirits.

- 1. Diagram of the Three Magic Circles

Below, the traditional model of the three circles is represented:

- Inner Circle: containing the divine names (Tetragrammaton, Adonai, Agla, etc.) and the symbols of Alpha and Omega with interposed crosses.
- Middle Circle: here are inscribed the names of the angels of the hour, the day, and the season, with their sigils and the designations of the time and the zodiacal sign.

- Outer Circle: presents the names of the angels of the air and their ministers, in the four quadrants, accompanied by the pentagrams at the outer corners.

Note: The visual representations should be copied manually with devotion and care onto previously consecrated parchment or white cloth.

- 2. Table of Days of the Week, Ruling Angels, and Ministers

Day	Principal Angel	Auxiliary Ministers	Planetary Intelligence	Planetary Sign
Sunday	Michael	Dardiel, Huratapal, Capriel	Nakhiel	Sun
Monday	Gabriel	Miel, Seraphiel, Damael	Malcha	Moon
Tuesday	Samael	Carrer, Tomim, Tarfiel	Graphiel	Mars
Wednesday	Raphael	Gabiel, Seraphim, Deliel	Tiriel	Mercúrio
Thursday	Sachiel	Castiel, Asasiel, Anael	Yophiel	Júpiter
Friday	Anael	Raphael, Rachiel, Sael	Hagiel	Vênus
Saturday	Cassiel	Machatan, Uriel, Sabathiel	Agiel	Saturno

- 3. Magical Hours — Division and Calculation

The magical hours are calculated by dividing the time between sunrise and sunset into 12 parts (diurnal hours), and the time between sunset and the next sunrise into another 12 parts (nocturnal hours).

Each hour has a planetary ruler, according to the sequence: Saturn, Jupiter, Mars, Sun, Venus, Mercury, Moon (repeating the cycle).

For proper use:
- Utilize sunrise/sunset tables for your location.
- Calculate the duration of the magical hours for each day.
- Verify which spirit rules the desired hour based on the sequence above.
- 4. Table of Seasons, Elements, and Heads of the Zodiac
-

Season	Element	Head of the Sign	Spirit of the Earth	Associated Symbols
Spring	Air	Aries	Oriens	Green, flowers
Summer	Fire	Leo	Paymon	Gold, fire
Autumn	Earth	Libra	Egyn	Brown, leaves
Winter	Water	Capricorn	Amaymon	Blue, ice

- 5. Names and Translations of Formulas and Prayers

- *Asperges me Domine hyssopo et mundabor: lavabis me, et super nivem dealbabor* You shall sprinkle me, Lord, with hyssop and I shall be cleansed; You shall wash me and I shall be made whiter than snow.
- *Exorcizo te, creatura ignis, per nomen Dei vivum...* I exorcise you, creature of fire, by the name of the living God...
- *Fiat voluntas tua, Domine, sicut in coelo, et in terra.* Thy will be done, Lord, on Earth as it is in Heaven.
- 6. Models for Ritual Records

It is recommended that each operator maintain a magical diary. A simple model for a record:

Date: [Insert day, time, and season]
Goal of the Ritual: [e.g., protection, an answer, spiritual cleansing]
Conjured Entity: [Angel or intelligence invoked]
Sensations: [Temperature, light, sounds, impressions]
Responses Received: [Phrases, symbols, visions]
Conclusion: [Observations, successes, difficulties, feelings after closing]

This record helps to evaluate progress, identify patterns, and avoid unnecessary repetitions.

This appendix concludes the complete course of the practices of the *Heptameron*. With it, the reader is equipped not only with instructions but also with ethical foundations and visual tools to walk with safety and reverence.

May this book be a mirror of your highest intention, and may each circle traced on the ground be a reflection of a circle kindled in your soul.

Afterword

The journey traced in this book comes to an end—but, like any true spiritual work, its conclusion is not a final point, but a portal of transition. The knowledge presented in the preceding pages, extracted from the *Heptameron* and expanded by contemporary reflections, does not intend to offer ready-made formulas or easy secrets. On the contrary: it invites the practitioner to the constant work on themselves, to the silent listening of the invisible, and to the disciplined construction of a bridge between worlds.

Whoever has attentively journeyed through the sixteen chapters of this work has surely perceived that, more than techniques, rituals, and invocations, what is required is inner posture, ethical clarity, and spiritual honesty. Legitimate magical practice is not reduced to robes, seals, or words. It flourishes in the heart of one who seeks the sacred with reverence, who acknowledges their ignorance without surrendering to it, and who desires more than to control: desires to understand.

The *Heptameron*, as a classic grimoire, remains shrouded in symbols and mysteries. But when read with the eyes of the soul and practiced with humility, it reveals itself as a true spiritual ladder: step by step, it leads the operator from the rite to the spirit, from the gesture to the essence, from the formula to the silence.

If anything remains after this reading, let it be the commitment to truth. May every magic circle traced from this learning be more than a sacred space—may it be the reflection of an inner circle, kindled in the consciousness. May every word pronounced in a rite be preceded by a mature silence. And may the search for the invisible never obscure the value of the visible, of presence, of the common life that teaches us at every moment.

Magic, in its highest expression, does not take us away from reality: it brings us closer to it with new eyes. And if this book has contributed to this rapprochement—more lucid, more loving, more ethical—then it has fulfilled its mission.

May the celestial blessings accompany your walk.
In light and truth.

www.ingramcontent.com/pod-product-compliance
Lightning Source LLC
LaVergne TN
LVHW040043080526
838202LV00045B/3464